THE TAYLOR
GUITAR BOOK

THE TAYLOR

GUITAR BOOK

40 YEARS OF GREAT AMERICAN FLATTOPS

TEJA GERKEN

THE TAYLOR GUITAR BOOK
40 YEARS OF GREAT AMERICAN FLATTOPS
TEJA GERKEN

A BACKBEAT BOOK
First edition 2015
Published by Backbeat Books
An Imprint of Hal Leonard Corporation
7777 West Bluemound Road,
Milwaukee, WI 53213
www.backbeatbooks.com

Devised and produced for Backbeat Books by
Outline Press Ltd
3.1D Union Court, 20-22 Union Road,
London SW4 6JP, England
www.jawbonepress.com

ISBN: 978-1-4803-9451-3

DESIGN: Paul Cooper Design
EDITOR: Tony Bacon

Printed by Regent Publishing Services Limited, China

15 16 17 18 19 5 4 3 2 1

CONTENTS

THE TAYLOR GUITAR STORY

THE REFERENCE LISTING

" My goal has always been to make a better guitar than the ones I see out there. Even if they're mine. **"**

BOB TAYLOR, TAYLOR GUITARS AD, 1999

THE
TAYLOR
GUITAR
STORY

At first, Bob Taylor just wanted to play the guitar. He bought his first one for $3 from a neighborhood friend when he was nine years old. But though his interest in playing music continued, it was soon surpassed by a fascination with the instrument itself. He was already the kind of kid who took his toys apart to find out how they worked. Now he tried to improve his guitar by touching up the painted-on body binding—a process that turned into a much bigger job than anticipated, ultimately getting the guitar "to the point where it would have been if I'd just left it alone."[1]

A nine-year old kid playing and tinkering with a guitar in suburban San Diego, California, in the 60s was not particularly noteworthy. Except that Bob's determination and curiosity led him to sand down the guitar's finish to the bare wood in order to paint it again—not once, but twice—and demonstrated traits that later would make the company bearing his name one of the most successful and respected in the business.

Robert Taylor was born in Oakland, California, in 1955. His father worked for the US Navy, and the family moved to sunny San Diego by the time Bob was in third grade. With money tight, he grew up in a household where his father built the furniture, and his mother—a seamstress—sewed many of their own clothes. It was more common to make or repair than it was to buy or replace. By the time he got to high school, he was already quite skilled at tinkering and building things, and it's no surprise that industrial arts and shop classes became his favorites. Bob won a slew of awards for his projects, which culminated in a swivel-base jeweler's vise that he made in metal shop.

As much as he loved working with wood and metal, Bob kept an interest in playing guitar, and also he took note of the cool-factor that surrounded the musicians who played at events such as his high school's talent show. He began a weekly trip on his bicycle to check out guitars at a local music store, Apex Music, and ultimately was smitten by the looks and sounds of an Italian-made Eko twelve-string. Even though it was a budget model, the guitar's $175 price tag far exceeded his financial reach, and this led to plans to build a similar instrument himself.

Armed with Irving Sloane's book *Classic Guitar Construction*—one of the first on the subject, and used by virtually every North American luthier during the 60s and 70s—he spent most of his eleventh grade year building a twelve-string guitar. He used a friend's Yamaha acoustic as a model for the body shape, found a pre-fretted fingerboard at a local guitar shop, and used a spruce top, mahogany back and sides, and maple neck. Again, Bob's determination was demonstrated not only by the fact that he finished the project at all, but also in how he used his metal-shop skills to build necessary tools such as a side bender, for which he welded a mounting bracket to a piece of pipe that he would heat up with the element of a barbecue lighter. Simple and effective, this tool would still occasionally be used for custom bends in the Taylor factory three decades later.

Encouraged by the fact that he'd built a playable guitar on his first attempt, Bob decided next to build two matching six-string dreadnoughts, a project that would take up most of 1973, his senior year in high school. One of the guitars was for himself, the other for his friend and future brother-in-law Mike Dwyer, whose guitar had to be built with a left-handed setup. "I had a little production line going and kept those two guitars moving along nicely all year long," Bob remembers.[2]

His first twelve-string guitar and the left-handed one he built for Dwyer haven't survived, but the guitar he built for himself has. The instrument is kept as part of an informal museum at the Taylor factory, and inspecting and playing it today, four decades after it was built, it's impossible not to be impressed. Its fit and finish are crude, the neck feels awkward, and the ambitious abalone inlays were clearly far beyond Bob's skills. But when you consider that this was the third guitar that an eighteen-year-old kid had built using basic tools and extremely limited resources, it's nothing short of amazing that it has held up, sounds great, and plays pretty good. There are countless examples of less successful guitars built by people with more experience and more access to teaching material and higher-quality materials, a testament to young Bob Taylor's intuitive skill.

He did more than finish his course work and build that pair of guitars during his senior year of high school. He'd also gotten a part-time job working at a gas station, which is significant not only because it allowed him to work on his Honda CB350 motorcycle during slow periods, but also because it's the only job outside guitar-making he'd ever have.

Bob's path was almost diverted when he became interested in the banjo. He'd met Greg Deering, the future banjo manufacturing powerhouse, a couple of years earlier at a school talent show where Deering was performing with his bluegrass band, and the two had crossed paths on occasion since then.

Now he'd heard 'Dueling Banjos' on the soundtrack to *Deliverance*, and suddenly the instrument's pull was strong enough for him to purchase an inexpensive Vega banjo, to start taking a few lessons, and to put him well on his way to playing in a bluegrass band. But, of course, playing an instrument was only half the fun, and before long, Bob was building a new neck for his banjo. "It was my best work yet," he recalls. "The shaping of the neck was really good, and the inlays were well done."[3]

The hub of the San Diego stringed instrument scene during the early 70s was a shop called the American Dream run by two brothers, Gene and Sam Radding. It was a hippie-spirited communal place that consisted of a retail store and a workshop where several luthiers each had their own bench for doing repairs and building instruments. "I didn't set their hours," Sam Radding, the luthier behind the operation, remembers. "I just said if you're going to build this instrument, it's got to be done by such and such a date: you can use my tools or bring in your tools, and as long as you follow the dictates of how our instruments are constructed, there isn't anything I'm going to tell you to do or not to do."

Radding, who is eight years older than Bob Taylor, also had an early start building guitars, and for a similar reason—he couldn't afford the Gibson he wanted. "I was probably fourteen, and I was able to save up $125. With that in hand, a friend of mine and I went to Apex Music in downtown San Diego. Here was this little ES-125: single pickup, nice little guitar. It was for sale for $145. I went and got a salesman, and I said I have $125. Can we make a deal? He just sneered at me and said no. I turned to my friend Kenny, and he had ten bucks. I said let me borrow the ten bucks, and we'll see if he'll go to $135. He did the same

■ Bob Taylor is pictured (opposite) with the first guitar he made, a twelve-string with a body that vaguely resembled a friend's Yamaha. Encouraged that this was a playable instrument, he built a pair of six-strings, one of which he still owns today. Though comparatively crude, the guitar (right) still plays well and sounds good, a testament to Bob's intuitive skills. Within a year, he was working for the American Dream in San Diego, California, whose owner, Sam Radding (top) was eager to hire him. American Dream guitars designed by Radding (like the dreadnought, opposite) provided the foundation for early Taylor-branded instruments, built in the same shop in Lemon Grove, California (early Taylor employee Bob Zink pictured working there, above).

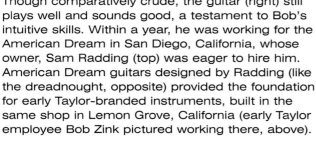

EARLY 70s *AMERICAN DREAM* DREADNOUGHT

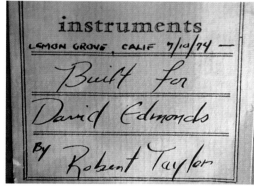

instruments
LEMON GROVE, CALIF 7/10/74 —
Built for
David Edmonds
By Robert Taylor

thing again, just really a nasty 'No!' ... so I turned to my friend, and I said I guess I'll just have to build a guitar. The guy looked at me, grabbed me by the sleeve of my t-shirt, and said, 'You don't build guitars, you buy 'em in stores!' A month later, I'd build my first hollowbody electric. A kid down the block saw it, and he said this is exactly the guitar I would like. I said OK, how about this. You give me $100 and supply the pickups, and I'll build you one. That was the start of the whole thing."

A few years later, Sam Radding found himself busy fielding orders for acoustic and electric guitars, for Appalachian dulcimers, and other instruments, and in 1970, he decided to go into business with his brother Gene, starting out in a shared retail space and workshop in San Diego. After a few months, the brothers discovered that working together every day wasn't something they enjoyed, so Sam found a dedicated workshop space a few miles east of the city in the suburb of Lemon Grove, while Gene kept the original retail location. Even though the two operations where now physically split, they continued to operate as the American Dream, with the retail shop providing most of the customers to order instruments. Just like he had taught himself the basics of lutherie, Sam Radding was now learning to refine his techniques for more of a production environment. "Bob Taylor and I are the only two absolute naturals I've ever seen," Radding says. "We might have looked at a book or something, but really only to say, 'Nice pictures!' I looked at a guitar, and I said there's nothing here that I don't understand."[4]

The American Dream would play an important part in the history of Taylor, but San Diego in general was home to a growing community of instrument makers: Greg Deering (who sometimes worked at the American Dream as a repairman), Larry and Kim Breedlove, James Goodall, and others were all planting seeds for their future successes. And the early 70s marked a crucial point for guitar making in North America. While the European guitar-making tradition had largely been about individual craftsmen working in small shops, perhaps aided by a few apprentices, the modern American steel-string guitar had for the most part been developed in factories.

For example, during Martin's golden era of the 20s and 30s, the company was already producing several thousand instruments annually. There had been exceptions, such as the instruments made by the Larson Brothers and John D'Angelico and by relatively anonymous builders whose reputation didn't go past their immediate geographic area. But the majority of desirable steel-string guitars had come out of the three major American factories: Gibson, Guild, and Martin. Now, there was a cultural shift. Acoustic guitars became the major instruments used in popular music, young men and women looked at alternative ways of living that suited their passions, and small shops sprang up that specialized in hand-made alternatives to the traditional factory-made steel-string.

On the East Coast, Michael Gurian and Augustino LoPrinzi were busy building custom instruments. In the Midwest, Stuart Mossman had started a highly respected operation. On the West Coast, builders such as Rick Turner and the Santa Cruz Guitar Company were emerging. And in Canada, Jean Larrivée was using his classical guitar making skills to develop a highly influential line of steel-strings. Still, even with the trend to small-shop guitars under way, it was tough to convince guitarists to consider buying a hand-made guitar by an unknown builder rather than a Gibson, Guild, or Martin—particularly when the build quality itself looked decidedly crude compared with the highly refined manufacturing that the factories were capable of.

However, while the guitars offered by the well-known brands continued to look great—especially to the untrained eye—there was no doubt that their quality had taken a downturn. Perhaps the big brands rested too much on past achievements, made too great an increase in production numbers, or too many changes in construction to reduce warranty claims. In some cases, using inferior-quality wood may also have been a factor. Whatever the truth, the late 60s and early 70s were not the glory days for Gibson, Martin, and other large manufacturers. (Perhaps because it had started later, Guild's quality stayed fairly consistent during this period.) It would take another two or three decades for small-shop instruments to be truly appreciated by large numbers of players, but these conditions did help open the doors for individual entrepreneurs looking to satisfy discerning customers.

Bob Taylor had discovered the American Dream while building his three high-school guitars, and he'd purchased some woods and parts from them. Following his graduation from high school, he began hanging out at the shop a bit more, showing Sam Radding and his crew the guitars he'd built, as well as a banjo neck he was working on. Impressed with Bob's skills, Radding offered him a bench, an invitation that Bob was excited to accept in the fall of 1973, following a post-graduation road trip. "My first impression of Bob was oh, he can have a bench in my shop any time he wants," Radding remembers. "He was well beyond where he should have been, had he been a normal person. When he brought in the first instrument I looked at, he was very reticent to say it had any quality at all, and I was looking at it going: well, this kid knows what he's doing. He's a natural on steroids!"

By the time Bob got set up at the American Dream, it had become clear that building guitars was going to be more than a passing passion. Announcing to his parents that he wasn't going to go to college but was going to become a professional luthier, he jumped into his new gig with both feet, starting work on a guitar on his first day at the shop.

For his first three guitars, Bob had adapted techniques from Sloane's book, copied elements from guitars he'd seen, and just made things work somehow. They were impressive exercises of rudimentary skills following a thriving passion. But even though he was to work independently at the American Dream, he was still expected to follow designs and building styles developed by Radding. This gave him a renewed sense of focus, and he would incorporate many of the concepts and lessons he learned then into his own instruments for years to come.

The American Dream built whatever its customers wanted, but Radding had developed his own take on dreadnought and jumbo steel-string flattops, loosely based on Martin's and Gibson's shapes, respectively, and primarily it was these guitars that came off the work benches at American Dream. Radding remembers: "Basically, the jumbo was looking at

EARLY 70s *AMERICAN DREAM JUMBO*

EARLY 70s *AMERICAN DREAM DREADNOUGHT*

THE TAYLOR GUITAR BOOK

1975 *TAYLOR DREADNOUGHT*

■ Sam Radding's American Dream Jumbo model (example pictured opposite, top) was inspired by the general dimensions of Gibson's J-200 model. But Radding built his Jumbo with lighter bracing, and as a result it had a sound of its own. Taylor would continue to build jumbos with the same body shape until 2013, and this has made it the longest-lasting design whose lineage can be traced back to the American Dream shop. Taylor also occasionally used a version of its unique mustache bridge, seen on the American Dream Jumbo, until 1997. Similarly, the American Dream maple dreadnought (pictured left) and the early walnut Taylor dreadnought (above) illustrate how Taylor essentially continued to build minimally modified American Dream models after Bob Taylor and Kurt Listug and their early partner Steve Schemmer acquired the business from Radding in 1974. Listug is seen (top picture) working on a batch of necks at Taylor's Lemon Grove shop in 1975.

Gibson J-200s, and going: why do these things just not perform? I was saying well, I could put these braces here, lighten up on the edges, make the instrument lighter overall; don't put massive pickguards on, don't use a thick finish, and select a really nice spruce top. The first one I did of the jumbo series was a very nice guitar. The dreadnought was more a look at a Martin, although the Martins were much higher-quality instruments. I made some slight tweaks to the bracing, like what people are now calling forward X-bracing."[5]

To Bob, these guitars were the ultimate. "I didn't know anything about guitars," he says of this time. "I didn't know Martins, Guilds, or Gibsons; I could hear the difference between a bad guitar and a good guitar, but I couldn't hear the difference between an OK guitar and a good guitar."[6]

The significance of American Dream for Bob went beyond the fact that he was building guitars within an established shop. It was here that he met three important people: Kurt Listug, who would become his partner in Taylor Guitars and who continues in this role to this day; Steve Schemmer, a third partner for the first nine years of the business; and Tim Luranc, a builder and repairman whom Bob would hire early on and who still works for the company today. Bob also reconnected with Greg Deering, whom he learned from and shared ideas with, and the two would enjoy a decades-long peer-to-peer friendship.

Kurt Listug was more interested in guitars than his studies in German and philosophy, and he would drop out of San Diego State after his second year. He got a job at the American Dream just a short time before Bob Taylor arrived, when he learned that Radding was looking for someone to learn about refinishing instruments. "I liked working on things, and I liked music and guitars, and eventually a bench opened up, so I got a job there. Which is funny to think about, because I didn't really know how to work on guitars," Listug says.[7]

"Kurt was a friend of a guy who worked in the shop," Radding remembers. "I don't remember how the whole thing came about, but I think it was mostly that his friend said that he should be here."[8] In a similar fashion, Listug recommended Schemmer, a childhood friend, when another position became available a few weeks after he started at the shop. Listug's first impression of Bob, however, gave little indication that the two would end up in a life-long partnership. "When he started hanging around, he seemed kind of straight-laced, kind of quiet. Sort of kept to himself, just focused on doing the work," Listug remembers. "The rest of us, we were all long-hairs, and he was fairly straight. I don't remember whether he came by just to buy some binding and purfling, or whether he came by to show Sam something he'd made. He came by on his Honda 350 motorcycle, and he'd strap the stuff he'd bought to the back. Sam was really interested in his work, and I got the idea that Bob was talented."[9]

By mid 1974, not quite a year after Bob's association with the American Dream had started, Sam Radding decided that it was time for the next chapter in his life. His little company had built around a hundred guitars in the four years of its existence, and he was ready for a change. "It wasn't that I was ready to move on so much, but I was just tired of dealing with musicians," he says. "It was also a mind-set. I always said I'm not a guitar shop, I'm a person. I have lots of interests; I do a number of different things. That's how I was back then. I just got to the point where dealing with everything was difficult, and I just wanted some time."[10] At first, Radding was just going to shut down his side of the American Dream—his brother Gene pushed on with the retail store—but after several of his builders expressed interest in continuing the guitar-making business, Sam decided to entertain offers.

Listug, Schemmer, and Taylor were all interested in purchasing the business, though not initially in the ultimate configuration of the partnership. Even though Listug and Schemmer had already teamed up, their original proposal didn't involve Bob Taylor, who in turn was trying to figure out how he might work out a deal with his friend and fellow American Dream builder Jerry Pike. But when the time came to lay out everyone's plans, Listug's keen business sense generated a detailed business plan, which he'd drafted with help from a local organization called SCORE (Service Corps of Retired Executives), a move that showed both dedication and a knack for finding help when he needed it.

Listug's plan was impressive but it had one major flaw. He and Schemmer had become handy around guitars: they knew how to do certain building operations and could do basic repairs. But neither had built a guitar from beginning to end. Listug's father, who was tapped to provide some startup cash, pointed out that having an actual luthier onboard would be a good idea for a company that was going to build guitars. He suggested recruiting the best builder at the existing workshop as a partner. Despite the fact that Bob had only been at the shop for less than a year, he'd established himself as the most talented builder. So even though they didn't know Bob particularly well at the time, Listug and Schemmer approached him about combining forces. "It sounded pretty good to me," Bob says now. "Kurt was interested in running a business and I was interested in building guitars."[11]

Bob went ahead and decided that joining forces with Listug and Schemmer was a great option. He also tried to get Pike onboard, but Pike declined. He borrowed an initial investment of $3,000 from his parents, and Listug and Schemmer each put in $3,500, bringing the total capital to $10,000. The three partners met with a lawyer, and after paying Radding $3,500, which mostly covered the tools they got as part of the deal and some outstanding debt, they found themselves as the new owners of the guitar shop they'd worked in.

Then came the first unexpected surprise. It turned out that the transaction didn't include the name American Dream or the existing phone number, which stayed with Gene Radding, who continued to use both for his retail shop. The three new partners came up with the name Westland Music ("We thought it sounded big, like a conglomerate," Listug says[12]), which was broad enough to use for a retail operation as well as for building and repairing instruments. But it wasn't really a name that would look good as a brand on a guitar's headstock. Since they couldn't continue to use American Dream, they had to find a new name. The partners discussed using each one of their names and decided that "Taylor" had the best ring to it. And it was Bob Taylor who did most of the building, so it made sense to put aside any egotism and go with it. "We all agreed that Taylor was a great name for an American-built guitar, and that it sounded as good as Martin," Listug says.[13] And so, on October 15 1974, the newly

1975 *TAYLOR 815*

■ While the earliest Taylors were essentially custom guitars, the company wanted to be a larger manufacturer from the start. A model-naming strategy was an early task, although the rosewood and spruce dreadnought (above) called an "815" shows Taylor's three-digit code wasn't finalized immediately. (Dreadnought models would have "0" as the third digit.) This 1975 shot of Bob Taylor (right) shows the company already building guitars in batches rather than one at a time. A few years later, Bob built himself this 810 (below), which he played for many years and still owns today.

BOB TAYLOR'S PERSONAL 1978 *TAYLOR 810*

THE TAYLOR GUITAR BOOK

1975 *TAYLOR MAHOGANY DREADNOUGHT*

■ On Taylor's first day in business after acquiring the American Dream shop, a rainstorm flooded the workshop (top), so the small crew had no choice but to mop up before starting work. Perhaps the most significant design element that Taylor popularized for acoustic guitars is its bolt-on neck. The company later refined the design as the NT neck, but from the early days to about 2001, it used a simple butt joint with two bolts, as on this early 912c (above).

THE TAYLOR GUITAR BOOK

minted entrepreneurs opened the door to what was now their own shop ... and not much had changed. Tim Luranc stayed on with three other American Dream builders, Bob Huff, Bob Mossay, and Tony Louscher, and the crew worked using essentially the same tools. They even inherited some wood and other materials.

"The first day as Westland wasn't too different from the day before, when we were the American Dream," Bob Taylor says. "We made the same guitars, using Sam's designs."[14] The first task was to complete any guitars already started and to fulfill existing orders. The next and much more daunting task was to find new customers.

■

Bob Taylor, Kurt Listug, and Steve Schemmer may have set up on their own, but for now, the first guitars built under the Taylor brand at Westland Music weren't much different from American Dream guitars. "There was no vision," Taylor says. "The vision was to make guitars for a living. It didn't really expand beyond being able to sell a guitar that I was working on, and hopefully make another guitar that we could sell, too. It was as simple as could be!"[15] Listug concurs. "We were pretty dumb," he says. "We were really kids. Bob's friend Jerry Pike—who was going to be his business partner until he joined me and Steve— Bob had him making guitar bodies, and we were just trying to make some guitars. We didn't even know how we'd sell them. We hadn't thought about that part yet."[16]

The Taylor operation continued to build to Sam Radding's designs, using the methods he had taught them and making a few small tweaks early on, such as a slightly more slender headstock shape (but keeping the "three-scoop" top section of Radding's headstock). "I didn't know the difference between how Sam made a guitar and how somebody else was making a guitar," Bob says. "To me, it was just a guitar." In more ways than one, his lack of knowledge about historic guitar models and how they were made would serve him well, allowing him to develop his own construction methods and tonal signature. His high-school guitars had been dreadnoughts because he'd copied the body outline from his friend's Yamaha, and when he first saw Radding's jumbo, it didn't make him think of a Gibson J-200— because it would be years later until he actually saw one. "People say oh, I'm sure he was really inspired by a J-45, or a D-18, but no, it wasn't even on my radar. It was so not a part of what I was thinking," Bob says. "For me, all those guitars I made at American Dream ... I was just trying to get through it. I was just trying to get the top onto the sides, and the back onto the sides, and the binding on—and the thought of the design of it is something that evolved slowly."

Of course, it wasn't as if Bob hadn't had any exposure to guitars other than Radding's or his own. In fact, he'd bought a Martin D-18 around the time he started working at the American Dream, mostly because he was fascinated by its craftsmanship. "It just looked like it was so well made," he explains. "It inspired me, because the construction quality was really high. But when I played it, it wasn't wow, this sounds good—I wish I could build a guitar that sounded like this! That thought didn't go through my mind at all. I looked inside, and I thought, well, I don't see any glue in there, and those braces fit really nicely into the kerfing, and how do they put the binding on like that?" Bob sold the D-18 after owning it for about a year because he had bills to pay, but he says that it left an imprint in his mind about where he should be able to go with the quality of his own guitars.

For the first couple of years, Taylor offered a dreadnought and a jumbo, but there were no specific models. As such, every guitar was essentially a custom-order, with variances in the woods and appointments. "When we built a guitar, we would have a little ready-form sale sheet," Bob remembers. "We would write on it, for example: 'Brazilian rosewood dreadnought. With bow-tie inlays, ebony fretboard, Japanese birch neck. Maple binding, abalone rosette.' And beside each of those would be a price." However, it's important to note that Taylor's focus at this time was more on improving the building process than on tweaking the actual design. "The guitars were pretty consistent," Bob says. "I wasn't experimenting with every one. With each guitar, I gained a little more of an understanding, but even then, I wasn't trying to make the guitars sound better every time I made one. I was just trying to make the guitar *be* better: better craftsmanship, and so on."

The majority of Taylor guitars built during this early period used spruce tops and Indian or Brazilian rosewood backs and sides. But at a time when the large manufacturers were at their most conservative in terms of offering anything out of the ordinary, one way that a small newcomer such as Taylor could set itself apart was by taking advantage of some gorgeous wood options. Accordingly, walnut and maple were popular options for Taylor customers who wanted an instrument that was more distinguished in looks and sound.

More important, however, was the fact that even though Taylor had only built perhaps a couple of dozen guitars, the company was already getting a reputation for easy playability—largely due to the fact that Taylor's necks were more similar to the slim designs of a typical electric guitar than the chunky necks found on most acoustics of the time. Again, rather than attributing this design choice to some clever research, Bob says he started shaping the necks of his guitars the way he did because he didn't know any different, and because the Eko twelve-string he'd coveted a few years earlier had a thin neck. "All I knew was that when I picked that guitar up and put my hand around the neck, it felt like a pencil. It felt wonderful! So when I made my first guitars, especially at the American Dream, I just kept filing on the necks until they got small, and lo and behold, people would pick them up and say wow, this neck is skinny; this is easy to play. I'd say, 'It is?'"[17]

Continuing the American Dream tradition, Taylor was a production environment from the very start, so it was important to the firm to improve the workflow, update its tools, and develop ways to build a guitar more accurately, even when monthly production was still in the single digits. One area that Bob felt could be improved in order to make his guitars more playable was the neck joint. Today, he is often credited as the guy who made bolt-on necks an acceptable choice for an acoustic guitar. But here, too, finding a way to solve a particular problem had more to do with the approach than with consciously trying

2001 *TAYLOR 710*

2001 *TAYLOR 710ce*

THE TAYLOR GUITAR BOOK

2008 *TAYLOR 810ce*

1997 *TAYLOR 810 LTD*

■ These 710s (opposite) and the 810ce (right) illustrate how most Taylor models are available in several variations. A standard formula includes a base model without further prefixes, and a "CE" (or "ce") version, meaning "Cutaway" and "Electric," with the latter referring to an onboard pickup and preamp. While 700 Series models have always used a rosewood back and sides and simple appointments, some details frequently change throughout the Taylor lines, as with the wooden rosettes on this era of 700s, which frequently featured abalone or plastic rosettes. In many cases, modified appointments are also presented in the form of limited-edition instruments, like the 810 LTD (above), which has abalone purfling. Easy-playing twelve-strings have always been part of Taylor's success, and the Lemon Grove-era ad (top), featuring an 855 with a mustache bridge, shows that the company made special efforts to promote this particular instrument type.

to be different. Because he worked with a book that taught how to build a Spanish-style classical guitar, Bob's high-school guitars used Spanish-heel construction, a method where the bent sides are inserted and glued into slots in the neck block, before the back is glued on. This results in a construction where the neck and body essentially become one piece early in the building process, forming an incredibly strong bond between the two.

The downside of the Spanish heel is that is impossible to remove the neck once the guitar is assembled, which in turn also makes it very difficult to make adjustments to the neck angle. This is not much of an issue with classical guitars, due to their much lower string tension. But steel-string guitars tend to be more finicky about neck angle and frequently require adjustments after a few years, and so very few makers use the Spanish heel on this type of instrument. Accordingly, the neck joint used for traditional American steel-string guitars built by Gibson, Guild, Martin, Washburn, and so on has been a dovetail joint, an intricate piece of woodworking that's also used in carpentry.

On a guitar with a dovetail neck joint, the tapered tenon (or tail) part of the joint is on the neck portion, and it slides into a matching mortise cut into the body's neck block, similar to a puzzle piece. Dovetails are strong, lightweight, and beautiful (although usually you can't see how a neck is attached on a completed guitar). And while guitar necks that are attached with dovetails are typically removable, doing so is a tricky process that involves using special jigs and softening the glue using steam. Furthermore, achieving a perfect fit during construction—which will have a direct impact on the guitar's future playability—requires a lot of skill, and even adjustments during the assembly of the guitar aren't simple.

In Bob's case, coming up with a new neck joint didn't take a huge amount of re-engineering. He'd learned Sam Radding's way of attaching the neck, a method that used a simplified non-tapered mortise-and-tenon joint as a way to glue the neck and body together. The joint could be made on a table saw, which meant that no routers had to be specially set up, greatly simplifying the process. But Bob had already converted a friend's Guild to a bolt-on neck as a way to do a neck-reset, so he knew that it could work, and he soon decided to modify Radding's joint by bolting it with a pair of hanger bolts rather than gluing it. "I think I made one guitar with Radding's glue joint, and by the next guitar, I thought this is just too dang hard: I'm going to bolt mine on."

He used this bolted version of Radding's mortise and tenon joint for some time, ultimately modifying it further. Struggling to achieve consistent neck angles, Bob typically needed to make adjustments while he was fitting the neck to the body, a process he felt was made more difficult by the tenon. He was encouraged by reading David Russell Young's book *The Steel String Guitar: Construction & Repair* and decided to try bolting the neck flush to the body. "Young was more radical than me," Bob says. "He didn't even bolt necks on, he just epoxy'd the neck right to the guitar, and he was proud of it! I figured that if you could glue the neck flush, maybe I could bolt it."[18] Bob came up with a method that replaced his earlier hanger bolts with two threaded inserts in the heel of the neck, and the result was the neck joint used on Taylor guitars until the introduction of the NT neck in 2000.

"Because of that, I was able to start adjusting the neck angle for each individual guitar fairly easily as I put it on," he says.

Anyone who has been around guitars knows that buzzes resulting from poor fretwork not only are undesirable, but also can be incredibly frustrating to track down. With their slim necks and proper neck angles, Taylor guitars were already enjoying a reputation for being easy to play, but less-than-perfect fretwork frequently got in the way. "Sometimes they'd just be bad, so before I would ship a guitar, I'd say this one didn't turn out good, I should really refret it," Bob remembers. "I'd take the frets out of the guitar, when it was all glued up, and I'd do it like I was doing a fret job. So I'd refret the guitar, and think wow, I've fixed this guitar and it plays great!"

Bob started to think that perhaps installing the frets *after* the neck is attached to the body as part of the standard building process was the way to go. He was encouraged by a conversation with fellow luthier John Carruthers, who was working at Westwood Music in Los Angeles at the time. "John said, 'Every time I refret a guitar, they turn out great! You should always fret a neck after it's on the guitar.' We talked about it, and he convinced me that it's a good way to make a guitar, so I went home and did that."

A short time later, Bob met luthier Jean Larrivée and discovered that he also bucked the industry tradition of fretting the neck before it's attached to the body. More importantly than reinforcing that choice, Larrivée also gave Taylor advice on the type of fretwire to use. Bob had mentioned how he was struggling with fret ends coming loose, among other problems. Larrivée suggested that Taylor try softer wire and provided a contact at the Van Gent company in The Netherlands, whose annealed wire Larrivée was using. "I ordered some," Bob recalls, "it came, I fretted a guitar, and it was like oh my God! It was like magic."[19]

Taylor was already operating as a manufacturer, with many instruments in various stages of completion at all times, so the way in which the guitars were built was becoming as important as how they were designed. Bob was quick to realize the value of going beyond his kit of basic hand tools. "One of the first big milestones was a machine that we call the shaper," he says. "Greg Deering turned me on to it." Rather than drawing an outline on a piece of wood and then cutting it manually on a band saw, the tracer allowed the use of a template, shaping a piece of wood to identical dimensions. With this, Taylor could make parts like neck blanks, tapered fingerboards, bridges, and braces with great accuracy and less guesswork. "Greg taught me what a shaper was. He was a little older than me, and he was studying industrial arts at San Diego State, so he knew a little bit more about some of the methods of woodworking than I did."

The fledging company couldn't afford to just go out and buy a commercially-made shaper, so Bob began looking for ways to build his own. Eventually he found the necessary spindles in a catalogue. In order to construct the actual machine, he went dumpster-diving. "There was a guy behind us who had a shop that made Formica counter tops. He'd put a template down and use a router to cut a sink hole, and what came out was what he called sink cutouts. It was a piece of particle board with Formica on top, the size of a double sink. We used those for

2015 TAYLOR 610e

■ Taylor has always offered guitars with maple back and sides, and since about 1980, the wood has been associated with the 600 Series. Over the years, the 600s have had a variety of appointments and have been positioned differently in the lineup. Maple is always a popular choice for twelve-strings, such as this 655ce (opposite). For many years, 600s were highlighted as especially suited for amplified stage use. But in 2015, Taylor completely redesigned them (610e, above), voicing with acoustic tone in mind and using woods harvested in a sustainable fashion.

THE TAYLOR GUITAR BOOK

2001 TAYLOR 655ce

■ Neil Young (above) was an early fan of Taylor's twelve-strings, and when he began using an 855 on 1979's Rust Never Sleeps tour, he became the most famous artist so far to use a Taylor. Twelves were thus featured prominently in the company's catalogue of the same year (opposite). Taylor's 500 Series (510ce, below) has always been high quality, with mahogany back and sides and a relatively austere look. For many years, Taylor's high-level production models were in the 900 Series, but here, too, details varied. The 910e (right) features the "Cindy" inlay that Bob Taylor originally designed for his wife.

2001 TAYLOR 510ce

2014 TAYLOR 910e

everything! We'd get them for free from the guy, and we'd build things out of them: bench tops, work stands, fixtures, jigs, everything. I made the table tops for the shaper from those. I built a little stand, we got a motor from a junk yard, put a light switch on it, hooked up a belt, I got two $15 cutters and bearings, and next thing you know, I had two shapers."[20]

Even though a handful of employees came through the shop during the first couple of years to help out, it was primarily Bob Taylor, Kurt Listug, and Steve Schemmer who built guitars and ran the company. Everyone wore many hats, but the default process had Kurt building bodies, Steve applying finish, and Bob building necks and doing final assembly. Despite the fact that Taylor was barely surviving financially, it is impressive to consider that in 1976, two years into the firm's solo career, the trio of twenty-somethings managed to build 168 guitars.

With production going up, the team decided to do away with the Westland Music name and change the name of the business to Taylor Guitars. They also decided to stop doing repairs and selling parts, signaling a sharper focus on being solely a guitar manufacturer. As such, they wanted to define actual models rather than custom-built variations of the dreadnought and jumbo shapes. "We sat down and discussed for hours on end, days in a row, what the model names were going to be," Bob says. "Stuart Mossman had the Great Plains, and a bunch of models that were named something like that, and that sounded really good, but we didn't want to copy him. And by then, we knew about Martins and Guilds, and we looked at all those models. One day we said, why don't we name them in a series? Then we could expand."[21]

The numbering system that Bob, Kurt, and Steve came up with used three digits. The first designated the series; the second whether it's a six-string or a twelve-string (1 for six-string, 5 for twelve-string); and the last indicated the body size. Taylor decided to call the first series 800, indicating rosewood back and sides, white binding, diamond inlays, and a few other cosmetic details. Since the offerings included a Dreadnought, Jumbo, and Jumbo twelve-string, the first models were an 810, an 815, and an 855.

Around the same time, a serial number was added to each guitar. Not wanting to be obvious about the relatively small number of guitars that had been built up to this point, they devised a five-digit system where the first digit was the year of production since the company became Taylor Guitars, and the last four digits reflected total production. The very first number that was applied to a guitar was 10109, indicating the first year of numbered Taylor production (1 means 1976) and the 109th guitar made (0109).

Brazilian rosewood was still relatively abundant at the time, and Taylor started out using it for most guitars, but as production increased it became difficult to acquire in the required quantities at an agreeable quality and price. As a result, Taylor switched to using mostly Indian rosewood. This was not an unusual move at the time: Martin had made the switch in 1969, and many other builders were doing the same. Coincidentally, Taylor purchased its first batch of Indian rosewood from Martin, and the fact that it took several years to pay off the $1,200 bill was a cause of great discomfort to the young luthiers.

While the company's production at the time seems extremely modest in comparison to its later output, it had far surpassed the orders that could be achieved through simple walk-in traffic and word-of-mouth promotion, which was the way they had worked in the American Dream days. To deal with the reality of having to sell more instruments, Listug began taking regular road trips to visit guitar shops in the hopes of turning them into Taylor dealers.

However, Listug's role as the company's sales person cut into his time building guitar bodies. The three principals, driven by the reality of barely making enough revenue to stay in business, decided to try working with a distributor in order to reach a wider audience. Listug says: "To have enough dealers to sell to, the challenge was OK, you don't have any money: how can you travel to meet dealers and show them your guitars? In the first couple of years, we'd get around California. I could drive to LA, I could go to San Francisco. But we couldn't get beyond that."[22]

Taylor had been approached by an outfit called Rothchild Musical Instruments earlier in the year but had declined the company's offer. Now, however, looking at a bleak financial picture at the end of 1976, the three decided to see whether Rothchild was still interested, and eventually the parties reached a distribution agreement. Rothchild Musical Instruments was founded by Edward and Paul A. Rothchild and had been trying to carve out a niche distributing quality instruments and audio equipment made by small manufacturers. Paul Rothchild had been a successful producer at Elektra Records and, looking for new challenges, figured that he and his brother could put his experience in the music business to work in new ways. The firm had already signed up the guitar brands Alembic, Larrivée, LoPrinzi, Oasis, and Travis Bean, and it also worked with Furman Sound and Bartolini pickups.

Taylor had big hopes for rapid growth due to its newfound ability to get into more stores, and a decision was made to expand the standard line beyond the 800 Series. The team remembered some of the birdseye-maple guitars they made at the American Dream and decided to introduce a model that would sit above the 800s, logically called the 900 Series. Besides featuring gorgeous maple backs and sides, these instruments also included rosewood binding and more elaborate abalone and pearl inlay. As was the case with the 800s, the guitars were available in Dreadnought and Jumbo sizes and in six and twelve-string versions. Acting on promises of more sales if a more affordable model was available, Taylor also came up with the 700 Series, which had rosewood backs and sides like the 800s, but used much simpler appointments, which helped cut costs a little.

Part of Taylor's agreement with Rothchild included a guarantee to sell a certain amount of instruments to the distributor each month. Even though Rothchild took a considerable cut of the profit Taylor would have gotten if it had sold directly to its dealers, this arrangement seemed worth it. At first, at least, Taylor was very busy building guitars not only for the Rothchild orders, but also for orders from before the distribution deal was made.

However, the big success that was going to pull Taylor out of its financial slump never really materialized. Listug had been skeptical of the Rothchild deal from the start, and over the course of the next couple of years, his concerns appeared to have been well-founded. Rothchild

1984 *TAYLOR 512*

CHRIS PROCTOR'S 1984 *TAYLOR K12C*

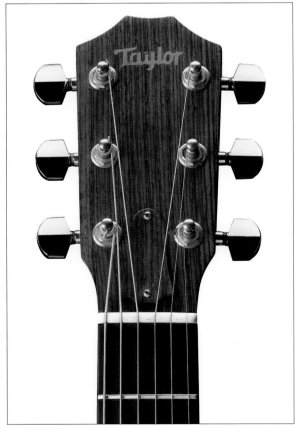

THE TAYLOR GUITAR BOOK

■ In the early 80s, although Taylor struggled to make ends meet, more top artists used the guitars, such as Nancy Wilson of Heart (top right). Taylor found some ways to make extra cash, like a consulting gig with Mexican luthier Francisco Andrade (right, with Kurt Listug, Steve Schemmer, and Bob Taylor, 1981). After a decade in business, Taylor introduced a small-body guitar in 1984, the Grand Concert size, developed with Chris Proctor. He got the first one, a koa and spruce K12C (far left, plus headstock detail). The size was soon offered in the standard line, some with an older-style bridge (like the 512 opposite). Proctor became a clinician, performing at Taylor dealers, and in 2000, the company built him a signature model Grand Concert (top left). This 712 (below) is an example of the Grand Concert size just before it was redesigned in 2004.

2001 *TAYLOR 712*

already had a lot of brands that were more established at the time, including Larrivée and LoPrinzi. And with a distributor in place, Listug was effectively removed from having contact with the company's customers. Rothchild was doing an OK job signing up new dealers, but it did little to support them once they were on board.

Rothchild also produced basic brochures—a first for Taylor—but its solution to slow sales always came back to requests for less expensive guitars, which led to the introduction of the 500 and 600 Series. Both featured mahogany back and sides (600s would later switch to maple). The 500 Series guitars were very plain in appearance, with unstained wood, rosewood fingerboard and bridge, and minimal appointments. The 600s were fundamentally similar, but the mahogany featured a dark stain, the fingerboards and bridges were ebony, and there was white binding. Introducing these cheaper guitars did result in increased production, but their smaller profit margins meant they did not lead to a healthier bottom line.

Despite the continuing financial woes, there were some positive developments during the Rothchild era. Perhaps most importantly, being represented by the same distributor as Larrivée and LoPrinzi meant that Bob befriended both Jean Larrivée and Augie LoPrinzi, who were several years ahead of his own learning curve. Taylor had been building guitars in batches, which seemed like it would be the most time-efficient method, because the same steps can be prepared and executed on multiple instruments. But building in batches also meant that if something went wrong along the way, the entire batch may be held up, resulting in a complete stand-still of production. Having gone through similar growing pains, LoPrinzi already knew that it was better to be able to complete and sell a guitar or two every day rather than ten or twelve every few weeks, and so he suggested that Taylor try that approach instead. Taylor decided to reorganize the shop into dedicated departments for the neck, body, and finishing, and to work in much smaller batches, aiming for the completion of three guitars per day. Ultimately, this new approach turned out to be a more reliable way to ensure smooth production, and while the number of guitars Taylor built would eventually increase, the fundamental concept of constantly completing instruments has essentially stayed the same.

Rothchild also brought Taylor to the annual NAMM trade show, which had the possibility of exposing the guitars to a lot of dealers. But because Taylor was only one of several lines of instruments distributed by Rothchild—including some other high-end acoustic guitars—this visibility was limited to how Rothchild chose to show the instruments. By the time the 1979 NAMM show came around, Bob Taylor, Kurt Listug, and Steve Schemmer were already fed up with their distribution agreement. Seeing their guitars in a dark corner of the Rothchild booth sealed the decision to terminate the deal, which they did shortly after shipping the final batch of guitars soon after the show.

Six years into their venture, the Taylor crew had to figure out once again how to survive. During 1978, its final year with Rothchild, Taylor built 449 guitars with eleven employees, but the profits barely kept the lights on. After considering the options, the decision was made to eliminate as many expenses as possible, which included laying off all the employees. Taylor didn't need as much space with just the three partners building guitars, so it stopped renting the second 1,500-square-foot unit it had started to use. The company even decided that it could do without business insurance.

Before the lay-off, Taylor was building about sixteen guitars a week. After looking into their building techniques, which included several time-saving procedures instituted during the growth of the last couple of years, Bob concluded that the three founders should still be able to build eight guitars every week. With dedication and long hours, the trio met its goal. "I was making the bodies, Steve was doing the finishing, and Bob was making the necks, doing final assembly, and then stringing the guitars up," Listug remembers of this time.[23]

Amazingly, by the time 1979 came to an end, Taylor had built 399 guitars. But with Listug busy building guitar bodies, the firm hadn't been able to reach the sales it had achieved during the Rothchild years. Sticking to their Everybody Does Everything mentality, the partners decided simply to divide their existing dealer list by three and to each take responsibility for maintaining the relationships and making the sales calls. The best thing to come out of this was for Bob and Steve to discover that being a salesman wasn't their strongest trait, while it became increasingly obvious that Kurt was a natural. They cut production significantly, because they didn't want to spend money on materials for guitars they didn't know how to sell, and the result was that in 1980 Taylor built only a hundred guitars. Rather than being a source of discouragement, the experience became a turning point, in more ways than one.

Listug figured that the best way to get new dealers to sign on was to hit the road with his Volvo station wagon full of Taylor guitars. "When we split from Rothchild, we had an idea of which stores sold our guitars, so we got on the phone with them and tried to pick up the relationship," he explains. "Then, when I went out on the road to call on those stores, I knew who to go to. I knew they liked our guitars."[24] At first, the trips were short, so that Listug could continue to contribute to the building efforts in the shop, but over the course of the next couple of years, his trips would become longer and longer. He'd be gone for weeks at a time, racking up tens of thousands of miles from coast to coast.

With Listug on the road so much of the time, Taylor hired Don Miller to fill in at the shop. With only three guys building guitars, procedural efficiency took on a new importance. Even though the shop was already well-equipped, mostly with tools that Bob had built, a lot of time was spent switching around various setups so that the same power tools could be used for different steps of the building process. With cash flow still a major hurdle, the solution appeared to be in borrowed money, leading to the decision to take out a bank loan for $30,000. Taylor still took a bare-bones approach to the actual equipment it bought, completing many of the machines with shop-made fixtures. But in the end, Taylor had a new shaper, resaw (a large bandsaw), dust collector, table saw, stroke sander, and buffer. "We created a few dedicated machines to make parts more or less on a daily basis, so we could just walk over there and do it, instead of making a big mess," Bob remembers.[25]

There were few new developments during the first couple of years of the 80s, other than further refining of manufacturing techniques and trying to stay as lean an operation as

■ While Taylor was still primarily working with grass-roots-level artists like Dan Crary, occasional brushes with superstars became more frequent, such as when Prince's band played a purple custom maple twelve-string (right) in his video for 'Raspberry Beret'. A growing staff had allowed Kurt Listug (above, in the shop with Bob Taylor in 1985) to focus all his attention to sales, which resulted in the company's first period of major growth. Taylor had also learned how to use the natural beauty of exotic woods to its advantage, as demonstrated with its all-koa guitars, such as this spectacular K22ce (pictured opposite, far right).

1992 *TAYLOR DCSM*

2005 *TAYLOR K22CE*

■ The flatpicking guitarist Dan Crary wasn't ready to let go of the Mossman six-string he'd been playing at first, but he did fall in love with a maple A55 twelve that he bought in the early 80s (below). By 1986, he was ready to talk about a signature model guitar, which was based on an 810 but featured a unique cutaway shape and straight instead of scalloped bracing. Early examples of the DCSM (Dan Crary Signature Model) had a Martin-style pickguard (see the 1986 catalogue page at far left), while the later examples (like this '92, above) had a standard Taylor pickguard.

possible. In 1981, Taylor got a small cash boost from a consulting job that took the three partners to Paracho, Mexico, where they were hired to teach local luthiers about advanced guitar-making techniques. As far as new guitars were concerned, Taylor reintroduced the 600 Series, which allowed for a broadening of the line without a lot of necessary adjustments to the workflow. This time around, rather than making a mahogany guitar that was fancier than a 500 Series, Taylor chose to use maple backs and sides for the 600s, providing one of only a few opportunities for a guitarist to get a completely blonde flattop at the time, while also creating the guitar's own tonal signature.

With Bob not only building guitars but also holding down the business end of things while Kurt was on the road, tensions began to build with Steve Schemmer. Bob and Kurt were starting to feel that the end of the tunnel was in sight, that their business was showing signs of improving, but Steve found it more difficult to be driven and optimistic. "Steve just wasn't getting his work done, and Bob was still staying up until 2:00 or 3:00 in the morning on Wednesdays and Thursdays getting the guitars ready to ship on Fridays," Kurt says.[26]

Toward the end of 1982, Kurt and Bob discussed their situation after Kurt returned from one of his long selling trips, and they met with a lawyer to figure out how to buy out their founding partner. Fortunately, the original partnership agreement included a buy/sell provision. Using the fact that Taylor Guitars had grossed about $100,000 in 1982 as an estimated value of the company, Kurt and Bob each borrowed $15,000 from their families to buy out Steve's shares in the company. After a few adjustments, in March 1983, the Westland Music Company had two equal partners, and in November of the same year, all assets were transferred into a new corporation, Taylor-Listug, Inc., with Westland Music ceasing to exist.

■

Nine years after starting their company, Kurt Listug and Bob Taylor found themselves at a new dawn of sorts. They still were struggling to make ends meet, but Listug's relentless treks across the country to sign up new dealers and sell guitars in person was beginning to pay off, the shop had become a highly efficient operation, and the two remaining partners felt a sense of increased control now they had bought out the third founder, Steve Schemmer.

Of course, while Schemmer's departure felt like a relief on the business side of things, the loss of his contribution to daily tasks in the shop required a replacement. It didn't take long for Bob to convince Tim Luranc, who had been at the American Dream and who was part of the crew that transitioned into Westland Music, to come back to work for him. Luranc had been working at Stelling Banjo Works in the interim, where he became a finishing expert, and even though he initially kept a foot in the banjo door by working only part-time for Taylor, he committed to full-time employment within a few months, and Luranc was still with Taylor at the time of writing (as of 2015, he runs Taylor's repair and service facility).

Also joining the Taylor team from the Stelling shop around this time was luthier Larry Breedlove, whose designs would have a major impact on the further development of Taylor guitars. With the exception of a several-year hiatus to form Breedlove Guitars (along with Steve Henderson, another former Taylor employee) in the 90s, Larry would remain part of the Taylor crew until his retirement in 2014. Combined with Listug's increasingly successful sales efforts, the addition of two highly skilled craftsmen gave the company a much-needed boost. By the end of 1983, the five-person Taylor team had built and sold almost 500 guitars that year.

It wasn't long after revamping the business structure that Taylor started to think about adding a new body shape to the existing Dreadnought and Jumbo sizes. It was around this time that the company was approached by a young fingerstyle guitarist who was looking for someone to build him a small-bodied guitar that had a responsive voice. Chris Proctor won the 1982 National Finger Style Guitar Championship at the Walnut Valley Festival in Winfield, Kansas, and he was frustrated with the available instruments. Large makers like Gibson, Martin, or Guild were not innovative at this time, and while a few smaller makers and luthiers had started to emerge, Proctor felt that many of their guitars either didn't sound as good as they looked or weren't stable enough to take on the road. Proctor recalls that when he won Winfield, they didn't have three good fingerstyle guitars to give away for prizes. "They had three dreadnoughts," he says, "and I was playing a dreadnought Mossman at the time."

Proctor had seen some of Taylor's instruments, and while none of the models that the company was making at the time seemed like a good match, he felt that if Taylor could apply its know-how to an instrument that he'd help design, they might be onto something. "Bob and Kurt were the only ones I could talk to," Proctor says. "I didn't have any cachet. I couldn't go to Martin or Guild and say what if you did this, what if you did that? But Bob and Kurt were my size, so they went ahead and built me a guitar."[27] Bob agrees with the assessment. "Kurt and I had been talking about it anyway, saying we want something that's not a dreadnought or a jumbo. Everything aligned, and that's really kind of when Taylor came more onto the scene."[28]

Proctor knew he wanted a wide neck, a cutaway, and a size similar to a Martin 000, but with slightly different curves in the body outline. The resulting guitar had a 15-inch lower bout, the same as a 000, but the upper bout was a bit narrower, creating a shape that's somewhat between Martin's 00 and 000 bodies. Taylor decided to refer to the body size as its Grand Concert, giving it the "2" designation in its model number system. Proctor's prototype (which he still owns) was a K12C with koa back and sides, a spruce top, sharp Florentine cutaway, and a wide neck that measured $1\frac{7}{8}$-inch at the nut. Taylor officially introduced the new guitar at the 1984 NAMM show with a 512 and an 812 (an optional Florentine cutaway added a C to the model). Later the same year, Taylor added the Grand Concert to its other series, offering a 612, 712, 912, K12, and K22.

Proctor's importance in Taylor's history goes beyond his involvement with the development of the Grand Concert. A few months after receiving his first guitar, he found himself touring extensively throughout the USA, often finding himself with open days between shows. "I was talking to Kurt, and I'm saying look, I'm traveling around doing

2001 *TAYLOR LKSM*

1996 *TAYLOR LKSM-6*

- ❖ Mahogany Jumbo
- ❖ Unique Cutaway
- ❖ Custom designed for heavier strings

Several years ago, Leo Kottke gave up the 12-string because he couldn't find one he was satisfied with after his favorite guitar was stolen.

Years later he stumbled upon a Taylor 12-String. He called Bob Taylor and together, they designed the 12-string Leo had been looking for. We named it the Leo Kottke model, one of our Signature Series.

The Leo Kottke Signature model 12-string is a beautiful mahogany jumbo body. The cutaway is smooth and under-stated. Its natural beauty is enhanced by the clean laminated wood binding. And the only fret inlay is Leo's signature in pearl at the 12th fret.

The beauty doesn't stop there. Wait until you hear it. The sound is powerful and definite—trademark Leo Kottke. The tone is well-balanced, top to bottom.

It was designed to be tuned down to C or C# and use heavier strings (the string pull is equivalent to a medium gauge 6-string set tuned to A-440); but plays well at pitch, without a weak hi-mid plink.

Leo is now playing at least 50% of his live music on the 12-string.

"Taylor involved me in every step of the design process. And after 4 years of work, I have a 12-string I can depend on for: tone, strong fundamental response, reliability (my prototype's been on the road for 3 years) and playability. It's a powerful, well-balanced instrument.

This is a *real* 12-string, built from scratch to be a 12-string."

Leo Kottke

THE TAYLOR GUITAR BOOK

■ In 1989, Taylor began making its own cases (below), ensuring a perfect fit and solving supply problems with third-party manufacturers. Featuring a unique look with a brown Tolex exterior and a purple velvet interior, the high-quality cases even became a powerful sales lure for undecided customers. A few years earlier, Taylor made a splash at the annual NAMM show when it showed a line of colorful Artist Series models (below right) that was eventually added to the standard line for several years.

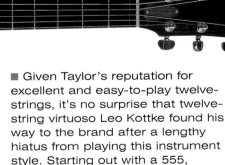

■ Given Taylor's reputation for excellent and easy-to-play twelve-strings, it's no surprise that twelve-string virtuoso Leo Kottke found his way to the brand after a lengthy hiatus from playing this instrument style. Starting out with a 555, Kottke eventually worked with Taylor on a signature model with a Maccaferri-style cutaway and lighter bracing, designed to be tuned low (C# was standard) and strung with heavy strings. The LKSM (top) was launched in 1990 and continues as Kottke's touring guitar of choice, even though the model was dropped in 2012. Taylor added a six-string version of the guitar in 1996 (left), and Kottke played both models during a concert at the Taylor factory (above).

concerts. You've got dealers out there, and you used to drive around and talk to them. What if *I* drove around and did these things?"[29] The result of the conversation was the beginning of Taylor's workshop program, which had Proctor (and later several other artists) giving a combination concert and Q&A session at Taylor dealers, providing a way to interact with potential guitar buyers and also to check in with the dealers themselves. Since Listug had cut back on his own dealer visits by now, this was a mutually beneficial arrangement, as it allowed Proctor to fill in otherwise open tour days and Taylor to nourish both dealers and end users.

Larry Breedlove's arrival at Taylor added a highly skilled luthier to the shop, as well as bringing his artistic eye and a background in fine arts. Accordingly, Breedlove was instrumental in the design of the Grand Concert shape. Perhaps even more far-reaching in its overall impact on the appearance of the majority of Taylor guitars to follow was his design of the trademark curved Taylor bridge, which replaced the earlier Martin-style bridge for most models.

Breedlove had taken classes on furniture design and finishing techniques, which included methods for staining woods using watercolors. He'd begun by experimenting on some maple scraps he'd found in the shop. When a carte-blanche order came in from Santa Monica's famed McCabe's shop that specified only that the guitar was to be fancy but not involve a lot of inlay, Breedlove suggested to Bob that he try using the method on a maple guitar.

The resulting maple dreadnought was nothing short of spectacular. The body was completely stained in translucent blue, which allowed the grain of the spruce top and the flame of the maple back and sides to show through, but also the guitar had stylized red, orange, and yellow flames painted around the soundhole, plus some restrained but sophisticated position-markers in the fingerboard. Even though the guitar was built as a one-off custom order, Taylor chose to bring it to the 1984 NAMM show, where it caused a stir. At a time when synthesizers, MIDI, and effects-racks were deemed more interesting than acoustic guitars, the blue Taylor received considerable attention, with photos in several trade magazines and a couple of guitar magazines.

Not surprisingly, the company started getting orders for similar guitars, which were initially treated as custom-builds. In a classic case of one thing leading to another, The Podium, a Taylor dealer in Minneapolis, Minnesota, that had done some business with Prince, came into the frame. Having already sold the local superstar a Taylor 555 twelve-string, Glenn Wetterlund, a store employee, had the idea to order a purple version of that model in the hope that Prince would be interested. Wetterlund's instinct was on the mark: Prince loved the guitar, which ended up appearing in the video for 'Raspberry Beret,' played by guitarist Wendy Melvoin. Given Prince's popularity at the time, getting a guitar into a heavily rotated MTV video was a big deal, and it helped reinforce Taylor's image as a modern acoustic guitar company.

The colored guitars were popular enough for Taylor to add them to the catalog in 1985 as the Artist Series, available as Dreadnoughts and Jumbos, and using "A" as the model number prefix (for example A10 for a Dreadnought, A15 for a Jumbo, and A55 for a Jumbo twelve-string). Available stock colors were blue, salmon red, charcoal gray, and green. Players who felt that that the flame-themed rosette was a bit too much could order the guitars with a wide single-ring abalone rosette instead.

One of the more unlikely players to end up with an Artist Series model was the bluegrass flatpicker Dan Crary, who purchased a custom A55 twelve-string in the early 80s. Based in San Diego at the time, Crary had been approached by Kurt and Bob about playing their guitars earlier in the company's history, but he wasn't ready to move on from his favorite six-string, a Mossman dreadnought. But now, impressed by the twelve-string, Crary showed interest in working on a guitar. As someone who plays with a strong attack and wide dynamic range, Crary typically preferred dreadnoughts that didn't have their top braces scalloped—all Taylor dreadnoughts did at the time—because he didn't care for the resulting bass response. (For the same reason, some bluegrass players prefer the straight braces of 50s Martin D-28s over the scalloped pre-war style.)

Eager to please Crary, whose playing he'd admired for many years, Bob went to work with his trusty 810-style guitar. Instead of the standard scalloped braces, he used taller, blade-shaped X-braces, which succeeded in giving the guitar stronger trebles and a highly balanced overall sound. On Crary's request, Bob also included a cutaway with the guitar, giving it an easily identifiable appearance. Crary loved the guitar, and Taylor, hoping to make inroads into the Martin-dominated bluegrass market, introduced the guitar as the Dan Crary Signature Model (DCSM) in 1986. Early editions of the model featured a traditional teardrop-shaped pickguard rather than Taylor's trademark shape, and a simple black-and-white ring rosette, further setting it apart from other Dreadnoughts in the catalog.

With Taylor's first decade in business complete, things began to look up for the company during the mid 80s. "We were making a couple guitars a day, and we had a really hard time selling them," Taylor says. "It was ten guitars a week … and one day, Kurt just figured out how to sell guitars after ten years. Pretty soon, we had all the guitars in stock sold, and we had the ones we were making sold, and we had orders for a month in front of us. We'd never experienced that before."[30]

It appeared that the weeks on end that Listug had spent on the road visiting dealers for several years was finally paying off, and when he decided to take a more aggressive approach to selling by phone, he was now talking to people with whom he'd established a relationship. "The hard thing is that when you're small, you have to wear a lot of hats," Listug says. "You can't just have one hat. So I had to do the books, I had to sell guitars, I had to pack and ship all the guitars every day. I was able to get myself focused enough to where I could have a certain time of the day where all I did was sales, or all I did was the books. Because it's easy when you do a number of different things to say oh, I'll work on this for a bit, or I'll work on that for a bit. As opposed to here's the amount of time that I have and I'm going to focus during that time on just that, and I'm going to clear my mind of everything else, and I'm just going to get on the phone and follow up on leads."[31] By 1986, it became evident that the

■ Taylor continued to build high-end custom instruments, like those Bob Taylor and Kurt Listug hold (above). But Taylor shocked the guitar world with its affordable 410 in 1991 (opposite). Mostly using the same design as other Taylors, built in the same US factory, and with simpler features, it was priced just under $1,000. The success led to further 400s, such as the 412ce (below). The original mahogany back and sides moved to ovangkol in '98, and as the 2003 catalogue (opposite top) shows, the guitars eventually received Taylor's standard bridge instead of the simplified pinless bridge originally designed especially for the line. Also in 1991, perhaps to distinguish the more expensive but similar 500 Series, Taylor introduced a limited edition of stained 510s (promo shot, opposite).

1997 *TAYLOR 412ce*

THE TAYLOR GUITAR BOOK

1991 TAYLOR 410

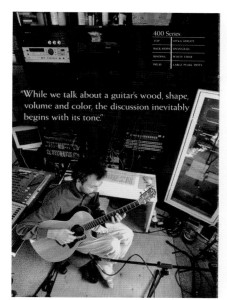

company would need more space, and when the year proceeded to go well, it looked as if a move to a larger facility was within Taylor's financial means.

Scouting for a suitable location, Kurt and Bob came across a new industrial-park development in Santee, about ten miles north of the existing Lemon Grove shop in San Diego. Once it was decided that this was the right place, Taylor broke ground on what would be a brand new 4,700-square-foot building. It allowed for plenty of elbow room, and it provided an opportunity to evaluate and improve each step of the company's building process. "It gave us a chance to start over with a production line that was fresh and new," Bob remembers, "to take all the ideas that I'd thought about for a long time, and to just start with blank paper and do it again. We had new workbenches, new bracing stations, a new spray booth, a new compressor—just a new infrastructure. Leaving all the stuff behind that had sort of grown organically over all that period of time, we were able to start with a clean slate."[32]

Once the move was complete, Taylor was riding a wave of success, and it soon became evident that Listug would need help on the sales side of the business. This led to the hiring of T.J. Baden, who started as Taylor's first sales representative and would go on to become Senior Vice President of Sales and Marketing. "The first year he was with me, we made a million dollars, and he was with me right up until we made fifty million dollars in 2003," Listug says.[33]

Around 1988, as the company approached the landmark of completing ten guitars each day, a problem that had been an issue for years became pressing enough that finally something had to be done about it. Taylor, like most other guitar manufacturers, had been buying cases for its instruments from a third party, and having enough cases in stock to ship completed orders was a constant challenge. Even when guitar production had been smaller, there would be periods when cases were suddenly backordered, meaning that finished instruments couldn't be shipped. The result was upset dealers, who paid their invoices later than necessary, and unprotected instruments taking up precious storage space at the factory. To make the matter even worse, getting cases that offered a perfect fit for Taylor's unique body shapes was difficult.

"We often had close to a hundred guitars waiting to be shipped, and a partial order of cases would arrive," Bob says. "We'd be dismayed at the awful quality, but our only options were to use the poor-quality cases and ship our production, or not to ship at all."[34] In 1989, he finally did what he'd been wanting to do for a long time, and he began to have his own custom-fitted cases made.

Doing so for the quantities that would be needed was no small undertaking. It started with the fact that the firm would have to rent an additional building just to house case production. "Unlike guitars, you can't build a case company without using some impressive tooling," Bob says. "All the molds for making the carcass have to be built, along with elaborate glue-spreading devices. The interiors of the cases require special glues, made from animal hides and applied with special machines. We needed riveting machines and big sewing machines that are strong enough to sew through the quarter-inch-thick hard plywood."[35]

Rather than reinventing the wheel, Taylor designed a case that used traditional five-ply wood construction with an arched lid and quality hardware. The cases provided a glove-like fit for each one of Taylor's body sizes, and their distinctive brown Tolex covering and purple interior lining was far classier than any third-party cases could offer. Providing its own cases not only solved a supply problem, but also it added value to Taylor's guitars.

One of the final projects to come Taylor's way before the end of the 80s was a celebrated collaboration with the fingerstyle star Leo Kottke. Kottke had released his landmark album *6 And 12-String Guitar* in 1969, and it put him on the map as one of the finest twelve-string players around. A couple of decades of his ferocious fingerpicking had taken their toll, and by the mid 80s, Kottke had physical issues with his wrist and arm that had him leaving his Gibson B-45-12 and Bozo twelve-strings in their cases and focusing instead on his easier-to-play six-strings. Kottke hadn't used a twelve-string on stage for several years when he came across a Taylor 555, and he discovered that the guitar's playability allowed him to play pain-free. Much to the delight of his fans, he decided that he could once again feature a twelve-string during his shows. Having caught wind of the fact that its guitars had brought Kottke back to playing twelve-string, Taylor suggested that they work together on creating a signature model.

Kottke's requirements were not without challenges. Taylor had the easy playability part covered: after all, much of the company's reputation was built on this instrument type. But rather than tuning the guitar to standard pitch as most modern twelve-string players did, Kottke prefers to tune his down one and a half steps, using heavy strings, resulting in a tuning where the first and sixth strings become C-sharps rather than Es, but in the same intervals as standard tuning (though he does sometimes go to alternate tunings from there). Kottke had found that a lighter-braced top worked best for reproducing these lower frequencies, and he'd actually shaved the braces of his first 555 himself, using a pocket knife. Because the overall string tension was actually lower than a standard set of strings tuned to pitch, slightly lighter bracing actually worked for his setup without compromising the instrument's structural integrity.

Over the course of several prototypes built in the span of a couple of years, Taylor refined the bracing shape and tonal properties of the instrument, which used the company's standard Jumbo body and was built with Honduran mahogany back and sides and a Sitka spruce top. The guitar also featured austere appointments with a plain (no inlay) ebony fingerboard, simple binding and rosette choices, and a unique cutaway that was inspired by the Mario Maccaferri guitars used by gypsy-jazz players. "Taylor involved me in every step of the design process," Kottke said when the LKSM (Leo Kottke Signature Model) was released at the 1990 NAMM show. "After four years of work, I have a twelve-string that that I can depend on."[36] The LKSM became a major hit for Taylor, and even today, many twelve-string fingerstyle players consider the model to be one of the finest stock instruments available for the genre.

A few years later, in '96, Taylor released a six-string version of the instrument called the LKSM-6, which featured the same Jumbo-size mahogany and spruce body as the twelve-

2015 *TAYLOR 312ce*

THE TAYLOR GUITAR BOOK

KLEIN'S FINE FOUR-STRING FLING

...And They Sound As Good As They Look!

The beauty of a Taylor guitar goes beyond the surface. It's the shape and the bracing that provides a clear, well-balanced sound. It's the smooth, streamlined neck that makes it so easy to play. It's the quality craftsmanship and attention to detail that makes it complete. And it's the reasonable price tag that makes it affordable. See for yourself at your nearest Taylor dealer.

For a color catalog write to Taylor Guitars, 9353 Abraham Way, Dept. G, Santee, CA 92071.
For a color poster of this ad send $4.00.

■ The couple of years surrounding Taylor's 20th anniversary in 1994 marked a highly productive period. A new kind of confidence replaced the constant need to convince people to try a Taylor guitar, as in the 1992 magazine ad (above right) when it had still seemed necessary to say "And They Sound As Good As They Look." Taylor's pair of XX-RS and XX-MC anniversary models (above left) were limited to 250 guitars each, and the swiftly-selling instruments introduced an exciting new Grand Auditorium body style. Around this time, Taylor began to collaborate with luthier Steve Klein (opposite) on the design for an acoustic bass, which was released as the AB1 and AB2 in 1995 (far left). And in 1996, Taylor introduced the ultra-high-end Presentation Series (PS55, right), which was the first standard-production line above the 900 Series. At the opposite end of the spectrum, Taylor added the value-minded 300 Series in 1998 (below).

2001 *TAYLOR PS55*

THE TAYLOR GUITAR BOOK 47

string. But while the LKSM-12 was designed for heavy strings tuned low, the six-string was made for standard-pitch tuning. Kottke, who for his six-strings had been using a Taylor 510 as well as guitars by Martin and the Minneapolis luthier Charlie Hoffman, has toured with his matching pair of Taylor signature models ever since.

■

By now, Taylor had established itself as a major player in the acoustic guitar world, and the company was ready to roar into the 90s. In stark contrast to the synthesizer-driven 80s, the new decade would see a major shift in popular music that once again put acoustic guitars front and center, and Taylor was in a prime position to meet the demand and become a trendsetting force of its own.

By the end of 1989, Taylor was a well-oiled machine. The company had about forty employees, it offered a full line of steel-string guitars with three body shapes and a variety of woods and appointments, and it had cracked the magic mark of 2,000 instruments per year. Amazingly, even though it had long used non-traditional construction details such as bolt-on necks and had been unafraid to use non-traditional building techniques almost since day one, the company was still fundamentally building guitars in a similar fashion to other makers. This would change shortly.

Just as the 80s came to a close, Bob Taylor had started to learn about a relatively new computer-controlled milling technology called CNC (computer numerically controlled). Applied in many industrial manufacturing environments, CNC machines can be used to precisely shape materials such as wood or metal, based on a computer program. Basic CNC technology had been around since the 50s, but it wasn't until now that it had become flexible and affordable enough to use at a relatively small manufacturing scale. Being the self-professed tool freak that he is, Bob had heard of CNC, but it wasn't until 1989 when he had a conversation about guitar manufacturing with the electric-guitar maker Tom Anderson (of Anderson Guitar Works) that he began to realize that he could use it to build better guitars.

Anderson had started using a CNC machine built by a company called Fadal for various building steps that benefited from utmost precision, such as cutting fret-slots, and Bob knew instantly that there could be myriad uses for this technology in his own shop. Taylor ordered its first Fadal in December of 1989, thus starting 1990 with an expensive new machine that had lots of potential and a steep learning curve.

"I like to do as many operations as I possibly can when it comes to cutting or slicing a piece with a really high-quality tool," Bob explains. "Accuracy was one thing that I wanted, but I didn't look at the machine saying oh, I'm going to carve my necks. I looked at it as: if I buy this one machine, I can throw away these ten machines. I no longer need my drill press the way I used to. I don't need that old gang saw that I got from Bozo Podunavac, who got it out of the Kay guitar factory, and which I built and restored to cut fret slots in my fingerboards. I don't need my little shapers that I make bridges with. It was a universal machine that I could use to make any part that I could conceive of on my guitar."[37] He'd found a way to exit day-to-day involvement on the production floor while setting up the case factory a couple of years before, so Bob now devoted much of his time to learning how to program the CNC using a CAD/CAM application (computer-aided design/computer-aided manufacturing) called Mastercam.

During this period, Bob reconnected with an old acquaintance who'd built motorcycle parts in a shop a few doors down from the American Dream. Matt Guzzetta was a master tool-maker, not a musician, but he'd hung out with the American Dream gang, attended their parties, and had bonded with Bob over their shared love for tools, manufacturing, and motorcycles. In 1976, as Guzzetta was moving his shop, he traded his old spray booth for a model 815 guitar—a considerable boon for Taylor, as the company couldn't have afforded one otherwise.

By the late 80s, Guzzetta had gotten out of the motorcycle business, instead dedicating his time to developing and building a new longbow that he'd invented. Having caught wind of the fact that Taylor had purchased a Fadal, Guzzetta started coming around, hoping to use it to fabricate some parts. Bob realized that Guzzetta was a walking encyclopedia of tool-making and immediately tried to hire him, but Guzzetta was too busy with his own projects to want a full-time gig. However, the two agreed to have Guzzetta come on board as a part-time consultant, a role that would gradually widen in time, and Guzzetta assisted Bob in getting his new marvel of a machine integrated into production. (In 1992, Guzzetta would finally join the Taylor staff as a full-time machine and tool designer. He retired in 2012.)

In the beginning, Taylor's CNC efforts essentially duplicated procedures previously accomplished with more primitive means, but with greater accuracy and taking up less shop space. "For the first several years, we just used it to do what we already did, in the same way that we already did it, so it was like a Swiss Army knife," Bob remembers. However, it soon became evident that CNC wasn't just great for making guitar parts, it was also superb for making the custom tools, such as jigs and fixtures, used in other steps of a guitar's construction. "We started making tools with it as much as we were doing guitars," Bob says.[38] It wasn't long until the company purchased its second machine.

CNC didn't just allow Taylor to gain precision, it also made it possible to streamline certain manufacturing steps. Many of the Fadal's operations aren't actually much faster than doing a similar process using less advanced tools, but because the machine can be set up to work on multiple parts at once, it allows a firm to prioritize skilled workers. For example, once it's loaded with the appropriate wood blanks, a Fadal can shape several necks, bridges, or fingerboards at once, requiring no attention while the work is performed. Already riding a wave of increased demand for its guitars, Taylor was able to increase production of existing models, but also the gains in efficiency had Bob thinking about expanding the company's offerings with a more affordable guitar.

Making a guitar that more people could afford was significant for reasons beyond the obvious fact that it would allow Taylor to sell more instruments. If you took a look at the

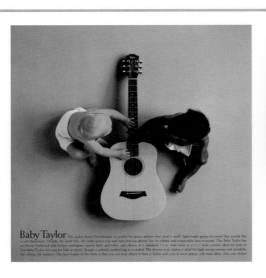

2015 *TAYLOR BABY MAHOGANY*

1996 *BABY TAYLOR*

■ Introduced in 1996, the Baby Taylor was an instant success. Not only did it invent the category of the high-quality travel guitar, but also it was an excellent instrument for children. Perhaps even more importantly for Taylor, the model provided a low-risk platform for experimenting with new designs and manufacturing techniques, many of which were subsequently applied to other Taylors. Introduced with mahogany back and sides and a spruce top, it was soon followed by an all-mahogany version (top). Over the years, limited editions of the Baby Taylor have included woods such as rosewood, maple, and koa, as well as a Liberty Tree version (right) and a Taylor Swift signature model (below, guitar on right).

2002 BABY TAYLOR LIBERTY TREE

acoustic guitar market in 1990, you would have noticed that no North American guitar maker offered a guitar for less than $1,000. As a matter of fact, it was difficult to find an acoustic guitar made from all solid woods at that price made anywhere. Rising labor costs in the USA combined with a flood of inexpensive Asian-made guitars by brands such as Epiphone, Takamine, Yamaha, and others had caused traditional American manufacturers of inexpensive instruments, such as Harmony, to go out of business, and for companies like Gibson, Guild, and Martin to focus on their more expensive models.

At the same time, with international currencies rising in value compared to the US dollar, some of the better imported guitars were actually becoming less affordable than they used to be, with quality-control not nearly as refined as it was on pricier instruments. Bob Taylor and Kurt Listug thought that if they could create a model that offered similar tone and the same great playability as their current models in a simplified package, and that could be sold for just under $1,000, it would fill a niche and have a huge market potential. "Bob got excited," Listug says. "He thought, you know what? I think I can make a guitar out of solid wood that we can sell for $998 with a case. I don't know what happened for him that he had that vision. He was probably thinking: how do I solve a sales problem? Because a lot of the ways you solve sales problems in a guitar company is you come up with a new model that gives you another thing to sell."[39]

About a year after adapting CNC into the manufacturing process, Taylor introduced the new 410 at the 1991 Winter NAMM show and immediately sent shock waves through the industry. With a list price of $998, the 410 was almost $200 cheaper than the 510, which had been the company's most affordable model up to this point. Taylor even included a version of its own high-quality hardshell case in the price.

Fundamentally, the 410 was a "real" Taylor. It used the same construction, bracing, geometry, neck-shape, and so on as other Taylor Dreadnoughts. It was built by the same team of craftspeople, and Taylor was careful to avoid cutting corners in the quality of the instrument. Partially, the savings were accomplished by using slightly less expensive materials. Even though the 410 used a mahogany back and sides and a Sitka spruce top, similar to what was used for the 500 Series, the sets used on a 410 might be slightly less cosmetically perfect. "When we first did the 400s, our spruce supplier was only supplying us with the most silky, beautiful tops you ever saw in your life," Bob remembers. "We were able to say, you know, if you have some tops that aren't as good as these, that we can buy for less money, we have this new model." Naturally, this also allowed Taylor to buy spruce in larger overall quantities, creating further cost benefits.

The 410 used rosewood instead of ebony for its bridge and fingerboard (but both were upgraded to ebony in 1996). Perhaps more important than the savings in materials were the reduced cosmetic appointments, which shaved off expensive labor time. For example, the guitar had simplified binding on the body and no binding on the fingerboard. It had a simpler rosette, basic white dots for position markers in the fingerboard, and even the Taylor logo in the headstock was made out of white plastic rather than abalone. The 410 also used a simplified, pinless bridge. "One of the things that took a lot of labor in the factory was when a guitar got into final assembly," Bob says. "You'd have to drill the holes in the bridge, ream the holes, cut the string slots, and adjust this and adjust that. Those people were pretty busy."

Bob realized that these types of labor savings would add up if the 410 really would lead to a significant increase in production, which of course it did. He was also aware of the fact that his staff was used to building higher-end instruments, and that it would take some adjustment to ramp up to the production he was aiming for. Relying on the Fadal allowed him to keep the focus of the skilled labor in his shop where it really counts. "I could run the Fadal more hours a day if I wanted, and I'll just design a bridge that when it's glued on, it's done: totally, completely done and ready to put the strings on."

Another hugely important aspect of the 410 was its satin (or matt) finish. By adding a satin compound to a similar finish used for its gloss-finish guitars, Taylor was able to eliminate the time-consuming final buffing stage, and in the process that meant saving time as well as eliminating a risky procedure that has the potential of accidentally damaging a nearly completed instrument.

Overall, the various time-saving measures added up to a 410 taking only about 65 percent of the time an average standard-line model took. "In real numbers, at the time, that probably meant about eleven hours for a standard model, and maybe eight for a 410," Bob says.[40]

Taylor clearly thought of the 410 as a somewhat separate line of guitars, and, perhaps in a fit of caution, created a unique serial-number sequence that started with the number 4 in front of a four-digit number (the first 410 was number 4-0001).

Not surprisingly, the 410 was an immediate success. In fact, demand for the new model was so high that Taylor had a to add a second work shift to build enough guitars. Later in the year, 400s became their own series, adding a 412 Grand Concert and an acoustic-electric 410e, and short runs were produced of a rosewood-backed 410, at first called the 410SE, for Special Edition, and later renamed the 420. When 1991 was over, the 400 Series accounted for about a quarter of the overall production that year of 4,800 guitars.

The era when, fundamentally, Bob built guitars and Kurt sold them had ended a few years earlier, but the exponential growth seen between the late 80s and the beginning of the 90s required not just additional help but also a look at what was working and what wasn't. For one thing, Taylor hired David Magagna as a dedicated Export Sales Manager, a move that would open up markets outside of North America. Magagna was an industry veteran, having spent eight years with C.F. Martin & Co., six as the US distributor of Lowden and Alhambra guitars, and two as president of Guild Guitars. "We did very small sales numbers outside the USA," Listug says. "David grew the international market: he found more people to buy our guitars."[41] Almost simultaneously, Rick Fagan was hired to help T.J. Baden on the domestic sales side, and the combined efforts resulted in a production increase of at least a thousand guitars annually for the next couple of years.

As the demand for 400 Series guitars went past all expectations, and with international growth and a renewed interest in acoustic guitars in general, Taylor began feeling the

2015 *TAYLOR 514ce*

2001 *TAYLOR 714*

THE TAYLOR GUITAR BOOK

■ Introduced with Taylor's pair of 20th anniversary models, the Grand Auditorium body had to wait two years to become part of the standard line, in 1996. While most of the resulting models shared the specs and wood combinations with other guitars within their series, Taylor chose to keep the XX-MC's cedar top for the 500 Series, and the resulting 514c (far left, with back) became a favorite with fingerstylists who liked the cedar top's quick tonal response. The non-cutaway 714 (left) was an affordable option for players who wanted a rosewood back and sides, but the model has also enjoyed the more upscale appearance of a sunburst finish (below). The 600 Series has maple back and sides (614ce, right), and the 814ce (bottom) is now Taylor's most popular model.

2015 *TAYLOR 714ce*

2014 *TAYLOR 814ce*

limitations of the Santee factory, only five years after having setting up shop there. An exhaustive search led Kurt and Bob to a largely undeveloped industrial park in El Cajon, just a few miles south of the Santee shop, where there was room to build a factory based on the immediate needs and space to grow in the future. Bob drew the floor plan for the new building, considering the ideal workflow for maximum efficiency. The resulting factory at 1940 Gillespie Way measured 25,000 square feet, compared to the 9,700 square feet of the expanded Santee factory. Obviously, the pair knew their company was going to grow significantly, but it's unlikely they could have predicted the enormous popularity that the acoustic guitar would gain over the next decade.

As Taylor began streamlining its manufacturing process yet again, one challenge was to focus on increasing production numbers while, ideally, continuing to elevate the quality of the guitars. "I think the quality of the guitars has gotten better and better," says Chris Proctor, the fingerstyle guitarist and Taylor endorser. "I like that attitude of yeah, we make really good guitars, but they're not perfect: and here are things that we're still bugged by."[42]

One step taken was to limit the available choices for custom work. While Taylor had previously offered various options for things such as binding, inlays, and finishes, these elements became difficult to track, and it wasn't easy for dealers to field many of these requests. Taylor continued to offer options as special-order items, such as cutaways, pickups, or different neck widths (Dreadnoughts and Jumbos came stock with a nut-width of $1^{11}\!/_{16}$ inch, and Grand Concerts measured $1\frac{3}{4}$, but either width was available, as well as the twelve-string's $1\frac{7}{8}$). A few years later, Taylor once again began to offer extensive custom options as part of its BTO (Build To Order) program.

In 1992, Taylor dropped the entire Koa Series from its line (although it would return periodically), as koa wood had become too difficult to source in the necessary quality, considering the quantities now needed to offer a standard model. Other examples of streamlining included the elimination of twelve-string Dreadnoughts in 1993 (although, again, some models would return periodically at later times), leaving the Jumbo as the lone twelve-string body choice.

Up to now, Taylor had been too busy just keeping the operation running to make a big deal of its anniversaries, but with the twenty-year mark approaching, it seemed fit to do something special. At a time when the company was thinking big in general, it was decided to go beyond simply creating a commemorative issue of some kind and use the occasion to introduce a completely new body size, one that would close the gap between the existing Grand Concert and Dreadnought (the only other size available at the time was the Jumbo). "We had said for a long time that it would be good if we had a guitar that was the length and width of a Dreadnought, but wasn't a Dreadnought," Bob says. "I'd conceived a guitar in my mind and had drawn a few shapes."[43] The goal was to create a highly versatile guitar that would be at home in many musical styles, something with more punch, bass, and volume than a Grand Concert, but better balanced and with more responsiveness to a softer touch than a Dreadnought.

As it turned out, the country music star Kathy Mattea was visiting Taylor during a tour stop in San Diego on a day that happened to be her birthday, and Bob spontaneously decided to offer to build her something special, using the new body shape he'd been working on. The resulting guitar was a black prototype of what was to become the Grand Auditorium model, which Mattea affectionately called Blackie, and which she played until, sadly, it was destroyed in the Nashville floods of 2010. Bob built a handful of other prototypes, of which he estimates that four or five were actually sold prior to the introduction of the 20th Anniversary model.

When the 20th Anniversary model was released to much anticipation at the 1994 Winter NAMM show, it was in the form of a pair of guitars that introduced the new body shape. The XX-RS and XX-MC were limited to 250 guitars each: the RS with Indian rosewood back and sides and a Sitka spruce top; the MC with mahogany back and sides and a cedar top. Rather than being loaded up with fancy decorations, the guitars featured relatively simple appointments. The fingerboard was left plain with the exception of a large anniversary inlay spanning the area between the thirteenth and eighteenth frets and a larger-than-standard abalone rosette. The bodies had standard black and white purfling, the headstock was left plain, and overall the guitars were more similar to a slightly dressed-up 700 Series than the company's top-of-the-line 900s. The idea, of course, was to fully highlight the new body shape, which in this first edition came without the distraction of a cutaway or a pickguard. Both models used premium woods, and while collectors quickly snapped up pairs with matching serial numbers, players immediately appreciated the new tone. Pick players enjoyed the volume and balance of the rosewood and spruce XX-RS, while fingerstylists found a completely new Taylor voice with the highly responsive cedar top matching the definition and bright tone of the mahogany on the XX-MC.

Even though the response to the Grand Auditorium body size was universally enthusiastic, it would be another full year until the size was added to the standard Taylor line. For 1995, Grand Auditoriums were offered as various limited editions, which were essentially similar to the anniversary guitars, but without the anniversary fingerboard inlay, and featuring a wider offering of woods. Besides a GA-RS (rosewood and spruce) and a GA-MC (mahogany and cedar), there was also a GA-WS (black walnut and spruce), GA-KS (koa and spruce), and GA-BE (Brazilian rosewood and Engelmann spruce).

Perhaps another reason that Taylor waited to integrate the Grand Auditoriums into the standard line was that there were other projects keeping everyone busy. For one thing, Taylor introduced an acoustic bass that was the result of a collaboration with the renowned luthier Steve Klein, a project that had started several years earlier. "I had met Steve at one of the ASIA symposiums," Bob remembers, referring to the bi-annual gatherings of the Association of Stringed Instrument Artisans. "He and I were sitting around, and there was the idea of making a bass. I said you know, Steve, I dig your designs, they're left of center, and I can never see myself making a guitar like the guitars you make, but they're certainly brilliant, and you're such a wonderful craftsman—but if I was ever to make a bass, the way you make a guitar

1999 *TAYLOR XXV-GA*

2015 *TAYLOR 414*

THE TAYLOR GUITAR BOOK

2001 *TAYLOR 614ce*

■ In 1999, Taylor celebrated its 25th year in business with a pair of special anniversary guitars. The XXV-GA (top left) featured the Grand Auditorium body that had been introduced five years earlier with the 20th anniversary model, and it quickly became Taylor's most popular body style. The XXV-DR, meanwhile, was a dreadnought. Limited to 500 guitars each, the models seemed understated for such a landmark, but the most significant element was hiding under the hood. These guitars introduced the new NT neck system, which not only made the guitars highly adjustable and serviceable but also allowed for more accurate production and a better yield from the woods used. Plain Taylor models such as the 414 (opposite) offer great value and are frequently used by professional players watching their budget. But Taylor has always offered dressed-up instruments as both standard models and custom orders: this 2001 cherry sunburst 614ce (above) comes from a time when the maple series offered a suitable platform for colorful finishes; while in this late-80s shot (top) blues goddess Bonnie Raitt is enjoying a Taylor Grand Concert model with custom inlay.

would be the way I would want to make a bass. Then he goes: why don't we collaborate? So he and I got together and designed that thing."[44]

Acoustic bass guitars have never been a huge market, but they had become increasingly popular as more bands wanted to use all-acoustic instruments on stage, whether for their entire sound or just an Unplugged-style set. Guild had some success with an acoustic bass design as far back as the 70s, Ernie Ball had introduced its Earthwood bass, and, more recently, Washburn had come out with an acoustic-electric bass that used a thin but hollow body and a piezo pickup in the bridge, bringing the experience of the modern acoustic-electric guitar to the table.

It's relatively easy to make an acoustic bass guitar that sounds good when amplified, essentially as a hollowbody electric bass with piezo rather than magnetic pickups. But it's tricky to build one with enough acoustic volume to compete with other acoustic instruments. The reason is mostly because the soundboard of a body that's small enough to be played on the player's lap like a regular guitar just isn't large enough to produce low-end frequencies in the way a traditional upright bass can. But Klein was known for getting an unusual amount of low-end from his flattop guitars, which tend to feature very large jumbo bodies (almost 19 inches wide at the lower bout on some models) and are braced and constructed according to the theories of the physicist Dr. Michael Kasha.

The Kasha design optimizes the soundboard's ability to vibrate by using a bracing pattern that radiates out from the bridge area and an asymmetrical bridge (wider and with more mass on the bass side than on the treble), as well as other design choices. Gibson built its Mark line of guitars using Kasha principles in the 70s, and there have been various makers of classical guitars who adhere to the design, but Klein was its strongest advocate for steel-string flattops at the time. Builders such as Harry Fleishman had experimented with applying the Kasha concept to an acoustic bass with promising results, so Taylor and Klein set out to come up with a new instrument.

The resulting bass was introduced at the 1995 Summer NAMM show, and it looked different from anything Taylor had ever made. The instrument's body was an enormous 19 inches wide at the lower bout and had a wedge shape, 6¼ inches deep at the treble side and 3½ at the bass, to make it more playable. Like some of Klein's guitars of the period, the design included an offset soundhole in the treble side of the upper bout, a choice made to allow for the maximum active surface of the vibrating top. The instrument's asymmetrical bridge was a cross between typical Kasha-style designs and Taylor's original shape, and Steve Klein's signature was inlaid in the fingerboard extension.

The bass was initially available in two models: the AB1, built with an imbuia back and sides and a spruce top; and the AB2, which used imbuia for the entire body. Imbuia is a South American wood sometimes known as Brazilian walnut. "The shape of the guitar and how it was constructed inside were Steve's ideas," Bob says, "and how we attached the neck and how we went about making it were mine." Both instruments featured a Fishman pickup. Eventually, Taylor added the AB3, which had maple back and sides and a spruce top, and the

AB4, which had an all-maple body. Although the Taylor bass was received enthusiastically, the high-end acoustic bass guitar market indeed proved to be fairly small, and by the end of 2002, the company decided to pull the plug on the instrument. "People loved that bass, and I thought it was a successful instrument," Bob says, acknowledging that marketing it was a challenge. "I figured out how to sell a lot things," he jokes about the project. "Get about a thousand of them in stock, and then tell everyone that you're going to discontinue them— then they sell in like two weeks!"

In the greater scheme of things, the bass served a much larger purpose than just to expand Taylor's offerings. By designing and building a completely new instrument, rather than trying new ideas within the context of an existing design, Bob was able to expand his own approach to his craft. "There were a lot of new ideas that stretched my mind. Just starting from scratch and tooling for something was a really good exercise for retooling my own guitars. I had an opportunity to start from blank paper, trying ideas for how to make something, totally different from the way I made guitars. And that allowed me to wonder how to apply these ideas to a guitar, but without changing the way a guitar looks, so that no one would even know that it was made this way by looking at it."[45]

Another instrument that proved to be highly important to Taylor's development was a seemingly insignificant three-quarter-size guitar called the Baby. Introduced in 1996, it wasn't just an attempt to create an affordable guitar for travel or to be used by kids, but, like the bass, it provided a platform to try out ideas that would ultimately find their way into virtually every other instrument Taylor makes.

Even though Taylor was already known as a company that used high-tech manufacturing methods to build a large number of instruments, the Baby Taylor's extremely stripped-down construction surprised many of the company's fans. They were used to Taylor as a maker of high-end instruments, not a miniature guitar that sold for well under $400. The spartan approach to the Baby's construction was immediately apparent to anyone who knows a bit about guitars. The body's top and back were joined with the sides without binding or purfling, and instead of an inlaid rosette, the guitar had a design burned into the wood using a laser. It had a satin finish, too, and as a particularly bold move, the neck was attached with a pair of visible wood screws that went right through the sixteenth fret. The guitar's back and sides were laminated sapele (an African wood often compared to mahogany), the first time Taylor had used laminated wood, and the back featured an arch, making it rigid enough to eliminate the need for back braces. Early versions of the guitar featured an unusual circular brace inside the body. Because Taylor thought that the biggest market for the Baby would be children, the guitars started out with an option of two available neck-widths, a standard $1\frac{11}{16}$ width at the nut, or a much narrower $1\frac{1}{2}$ inches that would facilitate small hands.

The Baby was an instant success. There had been small guitars before, but with the exception of some Spanish-made classicals or luthier-made custom instruments, the vast majority of them had been built with "cheap" as the primary design motivator. With a street price of a little more than $300, the Baby was no toy—it would take a dedicated parent to

2001 *TAYLOR PS10*

■ Although Taylor had built countless custom guitars using exotic woods and elaborate inlay, when the company introduced the Presentation Series in 1996, it was the first time that it offered a standard line above the 900 Series. Available in all body styles, the guitars feature a vine inlay spanning the entire fingerboard, abalone purfling, and premier woods all around.

2001 *TAYLOR PS12ce*

2007 *TAYLOR PS14c*

THE TAYLOR GUITAR BOOK

■ Taylor's Presentation Series guitars have featured a variety of woods for their backs and sides over the years. Early runs used Brazilian rosewood (as on the PS10, above, and the shot of the guitar's rear, right). But this wood has become not only increasingly difficult to procure, but also it is riddled with legal questions concerning its provenance. So Taylor has offered Presentation Series guitars in highly figured maple (far right), koa (the right-hand guitar, opposite), Madagascar rosewood, and cocobolo.

The ultimate expression in guitar making Brazilian rosewood's tonal excellence and visual brilliance inspire our incomparable Presentation Series. Bob Taylor hand selects the wood from our limited, private reserve and chaperones each guitar every step of the way through the building process.

2003 *TAYLOR PS14ce*

choose one for a small child—but its excellent playability and surprisingly mature tone meant the instrument led the way for a new travel-guitar category that would find other manufacturers scrambling to introduce something similar.

Even more than the bass, the Baby turned out to be a perfect vehicle to test various construction and manufacturing techniques before introducing them to Taylor's full-size guitars. For example, while the use of a two-piece neck and headstock was first introduced on the bass (where it meant that shorter pieces of mahogany could be used for the neck), the Baby took advantage of this design (which uses a finger joint to connect the two pieces) from a manufacturing perspective. Though much simpler, the Baby's neck joint represented a precursor to the NT neck that Taylor would introduce a few years later, as it was the first design that relied on screws alone, rather than bolting on the heel and gluing the fingerboard extension to the top.

"The Baby was a way for me, without any risks, to test some production ideas," Bob says. "I didn't have to put so much into it, because it didn't have to be ultra-refined, and there wasn't really anything to lose, because no one expected that much from that guitar. I was able to answer some of my creative juices." He says the Baby's neck joint is fundamentally similar to a simple Fender-style bolt-on, but it has to take account of the intricacies of an acoustic's much trickier geometry. He describes it as an awakening. "It's just super-accurate and really complex, but it fits in a way that you just could not do by hand."[46]

The Baby's neck-width option of 1½ inches turned out not to be as popular as the wider neck, so it was discontinued, and in 2001 the internal design was modified to eliminate the ring-shaped reinforcement brace. Baby Taylors initially shipped in fitting SKB hardshell cases, which where later replaced by padded gig bags.

A mahogany-topped version, the Baby-M, was added to the line in 1998, and by 2000, demand had grown so much that Taylor decided to establish a dedicated 8,000-square-foot facility that would just make Baby models. In 2005, Baby production was moved to the company's facility in Tecate, Mexico, where the instrument would once again provide a way to learn about production techniques before any full-size models were moved to this factory. Baby Taylors continue to be immensely popular, and over the years, several special editions that feature different woods have been released, as well as a number of commemorative and signature models.

Much of the work in creating new models, never mind refining the existing ones, happened parallel to a move that more or less reinvented how acoustic guitars are finished. In order to understand why this was a development of monumental magnitude, it's important to realize that finishing is the stuff that every guitar maker loses sleep over. Not only do most common finishes take anywhere from several days to several weeks to cure, resulting in production bottlenecks and the need to warehouse almost-completed instruments, it's also possible to ruin an otherwise perfectly constructed guitar if something goes wrong in the process. Like most manufacturers of acoustic guitars, Taylor had started out using nitrocellulose lacquer finishes. Nitrocellulose had become popular in the 20s, which means that it was used on the majority of guitars that are now considered to have been built in the golden era of vintage instruments. The finish came from the automotive industry, and because it was quicker to apply than the older varnishes or French polishes used on most stringed instruments up to that point, it quickly became popular.

Nitrocellulose lacquer has a lot of things going for it. It can be sprayed very thin; it dries hard; and if future repairs become necessary, existing and newly applied coats "melt" together, enabling invisible touch-ups. But there are also plenty of downsides. From a manufacturing perspective, the drying time of up to several days is the biggest issue, and due to the need for dust-free storage of partially finished instruments, this becomes a larger and larger problem as production increases—imagine needing to store several hundred guitars in various stages of lacquer curing.

Another issue is that, once cured, nitrocellulose lacquer remains sensitive to temperature fluctuations, especially if it warms up too quickly after being exposed to cold. Anyone who has seen a guitar's finish crack after an airplane ride or after taking it out of its case in a heated room following a ride in a car's trunk in the winter knows what that's all about. Finally, perhaps the most important strike against nitrocellulose lacquer is the fact that it is highly toxic. This is not only an issue for those in contact with the finish, but by the early 90s, California's environmental laws had made it virtually impossible for an operation of Taylor's size to continue using the material.

Taylor began experimenting with alternative finishes as early as 1976, when it started using a catalyzed lacquer finish for a while. Stelling Banjo was using the same finish, which used an added catalyst to help with the drying process. But after a while, the lacquer's manufacturer changed the formula, resulting in the finish being too brittle and leading to near disaster when guitars started coming back with cracked finishes.

Tim Luranc was one of Taylor's original employees, but he'd left to work for Stelling Banjo, where he ran the finish department. Taylor hired Luranc again in 1983, at a time when Taylor was gaining new finishing expertise. Luranc had experience using Fullerplast, a finish typically associated with Fender solidbody electric guitars, but which Stelling was successfully using on its banjo necks. When Taylor released its line of colorful Artist Series guitars in 1985, it used the occasion to try a Fullerplast finish. Fullerplast is very hard, and so is a good choice for protecting a guitar without a pickguard. Luranc's experience with Fullerplast paid off, and the finish worked very well, and Taylor soon switched to the finish for the entire line. But Fullerplast still took a long time to cure, and with Taylor's production growing, the perpetual search for a new and better finish continued, eventually leading to polyurethane, which the company used for several years.

In about 1991, Bob went to a seminar on UV (ultraviolet) cured finishes, and in a similar way to when he was bitten by the CNC bug a few year earlier, he knew that he'd found the answer to the challenges posed by long curing times. While traditional solvent-based finishes rely on evaporation and certain temperatures to cure, UV cured finishes harden through a photochemical reaction when exposed to ultraviolet light. Complete curing becomes a process

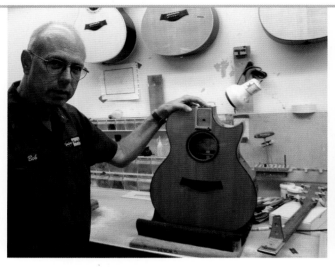

■ First introduced with the 25th anniversary models (below), Taylor's NT neck not only changed the way the neck and body were joined together, it also allowed for a much higher degree of precision in manufacturing, as well as the ability to use smaller pieces of raw materials. Consisting of a separate heel, neck, and headstock (seen here prior to assembly, opposite top), the NT design also facilitates easier handling in manufacturing, as the heel is glued in place after the fingerboard is installed and the neck is fretted (opposite center). These completed bodies show the receiving side of the NT system (opposite bottom). With the neck held in place by three bolts, adjustments can easily be made using special shims with varying degrees of angles (right).

1999 *TAYLOR XXV-DR*

THE TAYLOR GUITAR BOOK

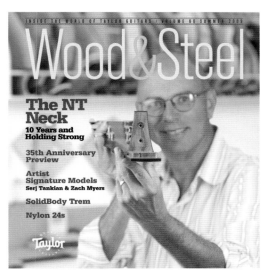

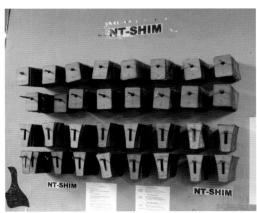

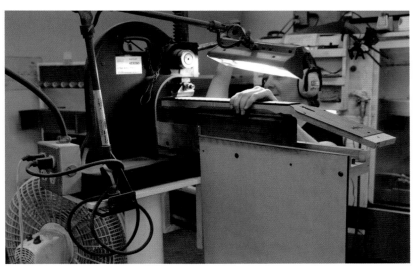

measured in seconds rather than hours or days, making it an ideal solution for a high-volume manufacturer. However, making the technology work for the unique requirements of building acoustic guitars was no walk in the park.

Because UV-cured finishes naturally enough require ultraviolet light, using the technology isn't a matter of just spraying a different type of paint. In order for the process to work, the freshly sprayed finish needs to be zapped by the light, which of course has to happen in a controlled environment. As with countless tools and factory fixtures before, Bob and his tool designer Matt Guzzetta got busy building a UV light curing booth which they called the UV Oven (even though high-temperature baking isn't part of the process), and with finish department manager Steve Baldwin they began an uphill journey of experimenting with the available options.

Making their way through virtually every UV finish available on the market, the trio began extensive tests on the various woods used on Taylor guitars, with initially humbling results. Sometimes the finish wouldn't stick to the wood. Other times it would form bubbles. Further tests wouldn't cure, while the next one might harden so much that the finish couldn't be sanded. Dissatisfied with the available choices, Taylor ended up taking his plea directly to the chemists who formulate the finish, and by 1994, they finally found an undercoat that adhered properly and a topcoat that cured just right. After a few more months of trials, Taylor switched to the UV finish in May of 1995 for its entire catalogue of guitars.

Having moved factories, introduced completely new instruments, and entirely revamped its manufacturing process in just a few short years, Taylor took stock in the mid 90s and decided to make various tweaks and additions to its existing line. In 1996, the Grand Auditorium was added to the standard line after being available only as the 20th Anniversary models and the 1995 limited editions that followed. This meant that there was now a model with the new body shape in all series from the 500 on up. Taylor chose the numerical designation of 14 for the body shape, resulting in a 514, 614, 714, 814, and 914, all adhering to the inherent wood choices, appointments, and so on for each series. With the exception of the 714, which was placed as a particularly bang-for-the-buck rosewood model, all Grand Auditoriums included cutaways, and the 514c kept the cedar top of the earlier mahogany-body GA editions, creating an instant fingerstyle favorite.

Taylor had put emphasis on creating more affordable instruments with the 400 Series, the Baby, and others, and so now the company decided also to expand its offerings at the high-end, creating a series that would be placed beyond the 900s. Of course, Taylor was no stranger to instruments that would fit this description, through custom guitars and limited editions, but the new Presentation Series, which was made available in all four of the company's then-current body sizes (resulting in the PS10, PS12, PS14, and PS15), represented a signal that Taylor remained a force on the high-end market. Presentation Series models have used a variety of woods in the years since their introduction, but the first edition featured Brazilian rosewood from Bob Taylor's personal stash for the back and sides, Engelmann spruce tops, and rosewood binding, paired with abalone purfling. Presentation

Series models also include a magnificent tree-of-life inlay designed by Larry Breedlove that spans the entire fretboard.

Now that Taylor had created two original body shapes—the Grand Concert and Grand Auditorium—it began to feel a need to modify the existing Dreadnought and Jumbo shapes, which had essentially continued Sam Radding's American Dream design for more than two decades. Taylor began by re-imagining the Dreadnought's shape, coming up with an outline that featured curvier upper and lower bouts with a slightly tighter waist, resulting in an original take on the dreadnought shape that pays tribute to both Martin's classic 14-fret design and Gibson's slope-shoulder body. Internally, the guitar didn't change much, resulting in minimal tonal changes. Updated Jumbo and Grand Concert shapes would follow later in the decade.

Seven years after the 400 Series turned upside down the perception of what an affordable North American-made guitar could be, it was time to revisit the line. Since its introduction, the 400s had quietly grown to include models in each of Taylor's body sizes, as well as twelve-strings and acoustic-electrics. But fundamentally, the series still adhered to the original concept of being a stripped-down mahogany-and-spruce guitar (although several limited runs had also been made with rosewood, maple, and koa back and sides). Several advancements in the manufacturing process had Taylor looking at ways to move the 400s closer to the standard line, with a new entry-level line called the 300 Series taking over the bottom-rung spot.

Introduced at the 1998 NAMM show, the updates found on the new 400s were easily spotted. Most significantly, the instruments' backs and sides were now built using ovangkol, an African species similar to rosewoods in appearance and tonal quality. The guitars now sported white plastic binding on the body and the neck, and with CNC production now churning out parts at a faster pace than just a few years earlier, the pinless bridge was replaced with the same pin-bridge used on other Taylors. Furthermore, Taylor came up with a new way to distinguish the line from the now common all-satin-finished instruments on the market by giving the top a gloss finish, while keeping the back and sides satin. "Now our inexpensive instruments looked the same from the front as our more expensive models," Listug says.[47]

Taylor fans who preferred the old-style 400s didn't need to mourn, as the new 300s essentially picked up the familiar territory. Now with sapele (a wood that's sometimes referred to as African mahogany) for its back and sides, the guitar kept a plainer appearance, with black binding, an unbound fingerboard, and generally simpler aesthetics. But the line also benefited from the standard bridge and gloss-finish-top updates, in effect continuing Taylor's efforts to create a high-value line of instruments whose low price didn't get in the way of professional-level tone and performance.

Taylor's success had the result that the company was once again feeling the squeeze of its facilities. Fortunately, this time around, there had been enough foresight to make sure that more room could be created by expansion rather than a complete move. As such, in the summer of 1998, the company began moving into a new 44,000-square-foot building that

2008 *TAYLOR LIVING JEWELS*

2000 *TAYLOR DDSM*

2000 *TAYLOR DDSM*

THE TAYLOR GUITAR BOOK

2000 *TAYLOR KLSM*

■ Taylor's relationship with its artists has led to many signature models. As with Leo Kottke, a design that started out as a custom instrument for fingerpicker Doyle Dykes turned into a standard model, as the DDSM (Doyle Dykes Signature Model, opposite, and Desert Rose limited edition, above right). Some signature models have only been short-run editions, such the all-koa Kenny Loggins KLSM (above and below). Even more eye-catching was the Living Jewels (top left) featuring koi fish inlays. A feature of many Taylor tops since 2008 is the relief rout (top left), with a small channel on the perimeter for a more balanced tone.

had been constructed next to the existing 25,000-square-foot facility at El Cajon. The new building was a two-story unit, and while the upper portion was primarily taken up with administrative offices, the bottom floor was Taylor's latest effort to build its most efficient factory yet, one that incorporated the workflow created by all the new technological advances it had adapted from scratch over the last several years. Settled into its new digs, the company found it was time to prepare for its twenty-fifth anniversary.

With the major splash created by the introduction of the Grand Auditorium for the twentieth anniversary just five years earlier, Taylor decided to celebrate its twenty-fifth year with a guitar that hid most of its innovations under the hood. Available in Grand Auditorium (XXV-GA) and Dreadnought (XXV-DR) versions, the guitars were built in a limited edition of 500 for each model. But other than an updated anniversary inlay between the thirteenth and eighteenth frets and a special wooden rosette, the guitars didn't scream "We're fancy commemorative models!" As a matter of fact, the guitars were built with sapele backs and sides—the same wood used on the entry-level 300 Series, albeit some spectacularly curly examples stained with an attractive caramel color.

While the 25th Anniversary models were restrained in appearance, they introduced the most significant innovation that Taylor had come up with so far: the NT (New Technology) neck. During its first two decades in business, Taylor had successfully paved the way for bolt-on necks as an acceptable choice for acoustic guitars, with high-end builders such as Breedlove, Collings, and Huss & Dalton and countless individual luthiers following suit. Taylor was now taking the critical neck-to-body juncture to the next level. Even though the firm's previous design already offered advantages in terms of manufacturing and future adjustability, it still required the fingerboard extension to be glued to the top of the guitar, meaning that it wasn't completely removable without the use of special tools and advanced guitar-repair skills. But Taylor wanted a design that would allow for even greater build-quality consistency, make future neck resets take a matter of minutes, and provide a more efficient use of woods that would improve playability even further.

Using lessons learned from the design of the Baby and the bass, Taylor came up with a neck that differed from the earlier approach in several ways. Let's start with the most radical aspect. Rather than use a combination of bolts that connect the neck's heel with the body and a glue to fasten the fingerboard extension to the top, the NT neck retains the two bolts through the heel but uses an additional single bolt to secure the fingerboard. This feature alone is significant, as it makes complete removal of the neck easy and allows the neck angle to be optimized through the use of tapered shims. It ensures that future neck resets are incredibly simple procedures and makes it possible for every guitar to leave the factory with a perfect neck angle.

But there are further ramifications that have a direct effect on playability. Most acoustic guitar necks end at the heel, leaving only the fingerboard to extend over the body. Even though the hardwoods typically used for fingerboards are very dense, this leaves a weak spot right at the highly stressed joint, frequently leading to a bump in the fingerboard where the neck meets the body (sometimes referred to as a ski jump). On the NT design, the mahogany portion of the neck itself extends past the heel and below the fingerboard extension, providing complete rigidity in every position.

Although it's referred to as the NT neck, the neck itself is really only one part of a greater system, because Taylor also had to figure out how to receive it at the body without changing the appearance of the guitar. What the company came up with is a set of two pockets: one for the heel; the other for the fingerboard extension. This is where Taylor's advances in using CNC technology came in, as it would be virtually impossible to achieve the incredibly tight tolerances required for the parts to fit together in a consistent manner without the help of computer-controlled machinery.

Besides the change in attachment, the NT neck also differs from Taylor's earlier neck in that it uses a three-piece design. This means that rather than being cut from a single piece of mahogany (or, on some models, maple), the neck itself, the headstock, and the heel are glued together from separate pieces of wood. This is not a new concept, as most classical guitars use three-piece necks, and some vintage Martins used headstocks that were grafted onto the neck. But in the context of contemporary steel-string guitars, Taylor was once again breaking new ground. Using this approach has two major advantages. First, it allows for a much more efficient use of wood, which in the age of vanishing mahogany is a major issue. But perhaps even more importantly, it also allows for much more precise manufacturing, as the neck can be worked on without the heel or headstock getting in the way.

Taylor began to experiment with a separate headstock on the bass and the Baby. For the first generation of the NT neck, the company adapted the use of a finger joint to merge the two pieces (and in 2007, Taylor switched to a cosmetically more attractive scarf joint). As a bonus, the resulting headstock was actually stronger than the one-piece design, effectively reinforcing one of the weakest spots on most guitars.

As for wood choice, the NT neck has been a game changer. Making a traditional one-piece neck necessitates cutting its side profile out of a large board thick enough to provide material for the neck's widest section. Of course, this board's grain has to be oriented the proper way, and because of the neck's shape, it's impossible to avoid a great deal of wasted wood, because of the relatively large areas left when the necks are cut from a board. With the smaller individual pieces of the NT neck, Taylor was now able to use wood cut into 4-by-4-inch beams, cutting out the required parts with a minimum of waste. The benefits go even further. Because of its even dimensions on all sides, the beam can simply be rotated until the ideal grain orientation is achieved prior to cutting the parts. And furthermore, because Taylor works with its own wood suppliers in Central America, sourcing these simple beams is a much easier and effective proposition than either importing whole tree trunks or having properly cut slabs processed on site.

After the initial run of 25th Anniversary guitars, the NT neck was slowly introduced into the full line, starting in 1998 with the 300 and 400 Series Dreadnoughts and completing the process when the twelve-strings and Grand Concerts switched over in 2001.

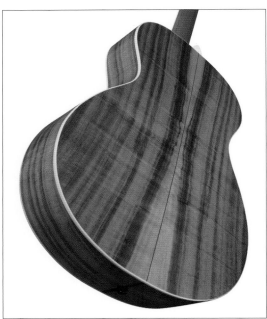

2002 TAYLOR LIBERTY TREE

■ In 2002, Taylor offered a limited edition of Liberty Tree guitars, which were made using wood from Maryland's Liberty Tree—the last of a set of tulip trees planted in each of the original colonies around the American revolution in 1776. Damaged by Hurricane Floyd in 1999, the tree was purchased by Taylor. The resulting guitars featured a patriotic theme, including a scroll of the Declaration of Independence that was inlaid into the fingerboard (top).

THE TAYLOR GUITAR BOOK

2002 *TAYLOR RUNNING HORSES*

■ Combining the skills of talented craft workers with the accuracy of advanced technology has allowed Taylor to create some outrageous inlays. The horse inlay in 2002's Running Horses guitar (left) was cut from koa, walnut, satin wood, and myrtle using lasers. The Rick Nielsen signature model (right) featured a three-dimensional "exploding checkerboard" design on its fingerboard, and the PG14 included an inlaid pelican set into the instrument's headstock (top).

2002 *TAYLOR RNSM*

Without a doubt, the 90s were a tremendous decade for Taylor, seeing the company's largest growth and many of its most original innovations. But really, those ten years simply set the stage for what was to happen in the new millennium.

■

No doubt about it: the 90s had been a defining period in Taylor's history, especially in terms of growth, branding, and visibility. Amazingly, the new decade continued these trends as the company offered a slew of new guitar types and innovations.

Perhaps as a way to recover from the intensity and impact brought on by the complete switch to the NT Neck the previous year, 2000 started out with refinements, modifications, and variations of existing instruments. Accordingly, Taylor's booth at the 2000 NAMM show was heavier on design than new innovation. Capturing visitors' attention was a line of limited-edition guitars called the Gallery Series, the first one of which featured an elaborate koi fish theme, as well as the first new signature models in a decade, with limited-edition instruments built through collaborations with Clint Black, Jewel Kilcher, Kenny Loggins, Richie Sambora, Doyle Dykes, John Cephas, and Chris Proctor. Of these, the Doyle Dykes model would later turn into a popular standard model. Taylor also introduced versions of the Baby that had maple, rosewood, or bubinga backs and sides, each offering a way to own a travel guitar with a bit more pizzazz than the standard sapele model.

Though outshined by the splash of 2000's limited editions, another guitar marked a significant point in Taylor's history. Logically called the Big Baby, the new model was indeed essentially a Baby that had been blown up. While the Big Baby's dreadnought-shape body was in a unique seven-eighths size, the guitar had a full 25½ inch scale. The Big Baby followed the Baby's simple construction cues: it had no binding or other fancy appointments and the same neck joint that attaches with two screws through the fingerboard. What was significant was the fact that Taylor was now a player in the under-$500 market, where it faced very little competition from other North American manufacturers.

With production of regular Baby Taylors already to capacity, and anticipating even further growth with the growing line of Babys, Taylor built a dedicated factory for just this series on its increasingly sprawling campus, a move that also created some breathing room in the main manufacturing facility.

The year 2000 marked the beginning of Taylor operating a satellite factory in nearby Tecate, Mexico. Located immediately behind the US/Mexican border, Tecate is only about forty miles from Taylor's headquarters and main factory in El Cajon, California, and for further perspective, Bob Taylor himself lives more or less equidistant from both locations. With Taylor bursting at the seams building guitars in El Cajon, freeing up space by moving its case production somewhere else was a logical decision, resulting in the lease of a 22,000-square-foot building in Tecate. Even though the proximity has the unique advantage of easy supervision and even the training of employees at the main factory, Taylor, faced with the possible challenges of operating in Mexico, proceeded with caution. "Guitar cases incorporate a high amount of skilled labor, and relocating the factory to Mexico allows us to establish a presence there without much risk," Bob said at the time.[48] Listug immediately saw the benefits of operating the company's own factory rather than subcontracting case manufacturing to an existing vendor. "With our own factory, we can hire and train our own people, and there's an opportunity, with the lower costs in Mexico," he says. "We went down and looked at Fender's plant and other people's factories in Mexico. We looked at Ensenada, Tijuana, and Tecate, and everyone liked the feel of Tecate—it's more of a small town, and very neighborhood-oriented."[49]

Moving an existing process to the new location turned out to be highly effective, and it met both goals of the experiment: to free up space in the main plant; and to lower the cost of case production without resorting to sourcing cases from a third party. Once case production was up and running, Taylor slowly began experimenting with the manufacturing of parts at the new plant, outfitting the location with the same CNC machines and other equipment that is found in El Cajon.

It would take a few years, but with confidence growing, the company eventually took the step to move production of Baby Taylors once again, this time south of the border and again using the little guitar as a test bed of sorts. As we'll see later, the Tecate factory today not only continues to build cases, Babys, and Big Babys, it also produces several of Taylor's entry-level full-size guitars, and it provides some of the internal parts used in the construction of El Cajon-made instruments.

Bob says that even though the Tecate plant is in a different country, it's essentially just a department of the main operation. "It's just thirty minutes away, and we have Taylor Guitars El Cajon management running the factory," he explains. "We drive in: we can go back and forth. We don't necessarily have to make an entire product line there. We can just make braces there; send wood down, dry it, sand it, send it back. We can do different things. And that's just one thing that we can do to keep the cost of our production down, because there are some operations that we can do there at a lower cost."[50]

Besides reshuffling the deck in order to accommodate the company's growth in production, back at the ranch, Taylor continued working on various actual guitar projects. Following a lengthy collaboration with the country fingerpicker Doyle Dykes, which had already resulted in a limited run of signature models, Taylor introduced the Doyle Dykes Signature Model (DDSM) to the standard line in 2001. Using a Grand Auditorium body with the shallower depth of the Grand Concert, the guitar combined maple back and sides with a spruce top, Gretsch-style position markers in the fingerboard, and custom-made LR Baggs electronics that used a hexaphonic saddle pickup with separate brass saddles and transducers for each string. Until Dykes moved on to endorse another brand in 2012, the model was a popular guitar in Taylor's line.

There were several developments in 2002, and one unique project was the Liberty Tree guitar. Built from wood sourced from the last standing liberty tree in Annapolis, Maryland,

2003 *TAYLOR NS74ce*

2002 *TAYLOR NS32ce*

2015 *TAYLOR 412ce-N*

■ In 2002, Taylor began to offer a line of nylon-strings. Rather than trying to be classicals, they aimed to appeal to players used to steel-strings. As such, they have Taylor's familiar Grand Concert and Grand Auditorium body shapes, narrower necks than a classical, and built-in electronics.

THE TAYLOR GUITAR BOOK

■ Taylor's new nylon-strings used a modified version of its Grand Concert body, mated with a 12-fret neck with traditional slotted headstock. The guitars were available in several of Taylor's existing series, including 300s (far left) and 600s (here, and controls, above). A Grand Auditorium version with a 14-fret neck was soon added (top, opposite). In 2013, they adopted Taylor's standard number system and received the same appointments as their steel-string counterparts, including fingerboard dot markers (as with the 412ce-N inset, opposite).

2002 TAYLOR NS62ce

which had to be cut down due to damage from 1999's Hurricane Floyd, the guitars turned an icon of patriotism into functional musical instruments. Originally one of thirteen liberty trees planted in each of the original American colonies, the tulip poplar tree had been the gathering place of patriots since before the American Revolution. "I would've given anything to get my hands on the wood," Bob says. "As a lover of American history, I was fascinated and moved by this tree's story, and I wanted that wood!"[51]

Getting a lead through a local guitar shop, Bob was ultimately able to purchase most of the salvaged wood in 2000, but as would be the case with any freshly cut wood, it took several months of curing before it could be turned into guitars. The original issue of Liberty Tree models came in the form of a Grand Concert guitar that used the tulip poplar for its back and sides (matched with a standard spruce top) and featured a patriotic motive involving the United States flag on the headstock, the scroll of the declaration of independence inlaid into the fingerboard and upper bout of the top, and a rosette that included the thirteen stars of the original colonies. Four-hundred of the guitars were made, and they were later followed up with a special issue of Liberty Baby Taylors and a batch of T5 electrics.

Taylor introduced a couple of new concepts as part of 2002's Fall Limited Editions, an annual and then bi-annual set of guitars that began around 2000 and that usually offer different features from regular models. The special releases in '02 marked the introduction of the first Grand Auditorium-size twelve-strings, which were first available in these variations of the 300, 400, 600, and 800 Series before in turn being added to the standard line the following year.

Taylor also introduced its "revoiced" Dreadnought as part of the 2002 Fall Limited Editions. Several tweaks were made to the guitars' braces and other internal structural parts, and these models had a boomier, more vintage-oriented sound than earlier Taylor Dreadnoughts (and the 510 and 710 LTDs even had chunky V-shaped necks). A version of these changes would eventually find their way into all of the company's Dreadnoughts.

Taylor also started using a technique called the Relief Rout on some model's tops. Essentially, this means routing a groove around the outer perimeter of the top (on the inside), close to the edge, a simple step that loosens up the flexibility of the top, yielding a more open and dynamic sound. Today, this technique is used on almost all Taylor models.

The biggest thing to happen in 2002 was, without a doubt, the introduction of Taylor's nylon-string models. Even though Bob had practically read himself to sleep with Irving Sloane's book *Classic Guitar Construction* as a teenager, his focus had always been on the steel-string flattops that were used by his musical idols. But as the music he was exposed to became more varied—in some cases due to Taylor artists who also played classical guitars— he became curious about actually building a classical guitar.

His first attempts were back around 1995, when he started experimenting with a few prototypes, some of which were taken to NAMM shows to show to artists and judge the public's general reaction. But as anyone who has an understanding of guitars knows, classical and steel-string guitars are two very different beasts. Not only is there the obvious, such as the fact that classicals have much wider necks, flat fingerboards, 12-fret neck joints, and different bracing than most steel-strings, they're also built much lighter: the lower tension of nylon-string guitars enables a different dynamic range but also makes it trickier to achieve good volume and rich tone. This is illustrated by the fact that, while many of the world's finest steel-string players use instruments that are more or less mass-produced in factories such as Taylor's, literally every classical guitarist performing at an advanced level will only use a hand-made instrument built by an individual luthier. The reason is that the tight tolerances necessary for a high-end classical guitar to offer an optimum sound are very difficult to achieve in an environment in which it's not possible for each instrument to receive a high degree of individual attention and care.

However, while Taylor's early classical guitar prototypes—which did indeed look like standard classicals with wide necks, traditional body shape, and so on—were perfectly nice guitars, they weren't game changers and didn't really fill a void in the market. But several artists, most notably the flamenco rocker Steve Stevens (best known for his work in the Billy Idol band), used the guitars during performances at NAMM, which meant that the cat was out of the bag, and Taylor kept trying to figure out how to successfully approach a nylon-string guitar.

Bob had no illusions about creating a guitar that a serious classical guitarist would choose. "We realized we had a lot to learn, not only about the guitar, but also about the customer and the market," he says.[52] He had noticed a growing number of guitars that combined the feel and playability of a steel-string with the sound of a nylon-string classical. Companies such as Godin, Lowden, Ovation, Takamine, and Yamaha were all offering these hybrid instruments, and he felt that Taylor should be a player in this market. These guitars were popular with jazz players, with sidemen who need a lot of different sounds at their disposal, and really anyone who wants some of the qualities of a classical without sacrificing the slimmer neck they're accustomed to from their steel-string or electric guitar. "I wanted a guitar that a player like me would pick up and instantly feel at home with," Bob said at the time. "Then, as the minutes roll by, you find yourself becoming more interested, rather than running out of steam."[53]

The resulting first edition of Taylor nylon-strings used a modified version of the company's Grand Concert body, with increased depth and a different cutaway shape, mated to a 12-fret neck that measured $1\frac{7}{8}$-inch at the nut, which put it between the full 2 inches of a classical and the $1\frac{11}{16}$ or $1\frac{3}{4}$ of a typical steel-string flattop. The guitars had slightly radiused fingerboards, a traditional slotted headstock (Taylor moved access to the neck's truss rod into the soundhole, rather than behind the nut), and an asymmetrical fan-bracing pattern inside the top.

Available as part of the existing 300, 400, 600, and 700 Series, the NS guitars adhered to similar wood combinations as their steel-string cousins, with the NS32ce and NS42ce using Sitka spruce tops, the NS62ce featuring an Engelmann spruce top, and the NS72ce using a cedar top. As the "ce" designations indicate, all models included a cutaway (c) and Fishman

BUILDER'S RESERVE VIII

Curve Appeal

A custom contoured cutaway adds a smooth twist to a beautiful figured walnut/cedar GS, paired with a matching walnut amp

1999 *TAYLOR W10*

2005 *TAYLOR W65*

2005 *TAYLOR W12ce*

THE TAYLOR GUITAR BOOK

CARE FOR A WALNUT, SIR?

2005 TAYLOR W65ce

■ Throughout its history, Taylor has been one of the few guitar companies to make extensive use of walnut. Domestically grown, walnut offers excellent tonal properties and can often feature stunning figure. Taylor has used the wood for backs and sides, paired with a spruce top (as on the W10, opposite top, the W12ce, opposite bottom, and the limited-edition Builder's Reserve VIII, opposite top left) as well as for the entire body, as on the W65 12-string (back only, opposite). Perhaps because it's less known than other more common woods, walnut guitars have proved to be difficult to market, and Taylor has periodically stopped offering the wood on standard models.

electronics (e). A 500 Series mahogany model (NS52ce) was added later in the year, and the company also started to offer nylon-strings using its Grand Auditorium body, building them without cutaways, as a reaction to players who wanted more acoustic volume than the nylon-strung Grand Concert platform was capable of. These Grand Auditorium nylons were added to the standard line the following year as the NS34, NS44, NS54, NS64, and NS74.

When Taylor first started building guitars, the inclusion of a pickup wasn't much of an issue. Ovations were the acoustic-electrics du jour, and if you actually wanted your acoustic to sound like an acoustic, you struggled with an external microphone on stage. Today, Taylor builds more guitars with pickups than without, but the company's full-on dive into plugged-in territory in the late 90s came as a surprise to many, as its previous stance toward acoustic-electrics had been a reluctant one. Like most smaller builders of high-end guitars, Taylor saw itself as being in charge of providing a great-sounding instrument, essentially letting others worry about adding electronics.

Part of the issue was that even though steel-string flattops with factory-installed electronics had been around for a couple of decades—starting with guitars such as Gibson's J-160E, and then later instruments made by Guild, Washburn, and others, in addition to the ubiquitous Ovation—they really didn't become widespread until the development of the modern undersaddle piezo pickup in the late 80s. Taylor offered the option of pickup systems almost from the very beginning. "The first pickup we used was a Barcus Berry," Bob says. "Then we started using LR Baggs, when Baggs was making the LB6 saddle pickup."[54] Eventually, Taylor switched to using primarily Fishman pickups, but until 1998 the company had a stance against the side-mounted preamps with volume and EQ controls that were becoming almost omnipresent in other maker's guitars. From '98, it began including Fishman Prefix systems in all its standard models with cutaways. Cutaway guitars were the most popular models in Taylor's lineup, and suddenly the company was one of the largest makers of acoustic-electrics in the business.

Taylors have long been the guitars of choice for countless performers, and having guitars readily available with onboard electronics turned out to be hugely successful. But as a company that likes to make things in-house and that also likes to innovate, it didn't take long for Taylor to start looking beyond buying the same off-the-shelf electronics packages used by its competitors.

Proprietary electronics were not unheard of. Companies such as Alvarez-Yairi, Ovation, Takamine, Yamaha, and others used pickups and preamps of their own development rather than relying on third-party suppliers. Using proprietary electronics not only makes it easier to achieve a signature tonality and to create a distinction from guitars by other brands that generally use the same electronics, it also means independence from outside suppliers.

For Taylor, the process of developing its own pickup system began in the factory's final-setup and repair departments. "We just had massive problems with the pickups we were using," David Hosler explains. Hosler worked in repairs and R&D. "We couldn't balance pickups," he says. "It was nightmarish, the number of guitars that we couldn't get out the door every day."[55] Frustrated by the state of affairs, Hosler one evening sent an email to Bob Taylor explaining the severity of the situation, saying that something ought to be done. "The next day, Bob came into my room and said why don't you do something about it? See what you can figure out!"

Hosler proceeded to educate himself on every kind of available acoustic guitar pickup and their histories, and he tried to gain a deeper understanding of just how a guitar developed its sound, where it came from, and what impacts it. He found an ally in Mark French, an amateur luthier and also an adjunct professor of structural dynamics at the University of Michigan. Hosler and French used the university's 3-D lasers, anechoic chamber, and other equipment to closely study the vibrations of a guitar's top. What the two learned was that an acoustic guitar is a much more complex mechanism than they felt could be accurately reproduced with the common undersaddle piezo pickups available at the time. Hosler took this knowledge, combined with the fact that he wanted to get away from piezos anyway, due to the installation challenges he'd experienced, and he began to search for alternatives.

Of course, pickups mounted under the guitar's saddle weren't the only choice available in the late 90s. As a matter of fact, while they had become—and continue to be—the most common type, many guitarists didn't like their sound, often describing the initial attack in particular as unnatural or "quacky." The most common alternatives were magnetic pickups that mount into the guitar's soundhole, and transducers (also often piezo-based) that mount directly to the guitar's vibrating top. Some performing guitarists were combining these options, taking advantage of a magnetic pickup's excellent bass reproduction and the soundboard transducer's microphone-like reproduction of body movement and high-end frequencies. Chris Proctor, who had long been involved with Taylor as an endorser, was a vocal advocate for this approach, as was the late Michael Hedges, who, for many acoustic players, served as a benchmark of a successful amplified sound.

But for the most part, combining multiple pickup choices—often using equipment made by different brands—required a somewhat adventurous spirit, as well as some additional equipment to mix the various sources, special cables, and so on. Hosler's experiments led him to a fundamentally similar approach to these cobbled-together systems, but not only did he come up with an unobtrusive and easy-to-use package, he also incorporated features and technologies that were new to acoustic guitar amplification.

Along the way, Hosler picked up a remarkable partner to develop Taylor's new electronics: the audio legend Rupert Neve, famed for his work with recording studio consoles, who agreed to consult on the project. "Rupert's coming on board gave us horsepower," Bob says. "He inspired us along the way and really was able to take David's inventive fervor down this long path of experimentation."[56] Neve designed the system's onboard preamp, suggested using magnetic pickup technology all around, and was in favor of making the system low-impedance.

Ultimately, the ES or Expression System had three pickups. One was fundamentally similar to a standard electric guitar pickup in that it had a wire coil wrapped around a magnet

2007 *TAYLOR 214e*

■ By the mid 2000s, Taylor's existing entry-level 300 and 400 Series guitars had slowly crept well past the $1,000 price point that had been their original target. Accordingly, a new line was needed, and it was introduced as the 110 (a cutaway version is pictured, below) and the 214 (top) in 2007. They were the first full-size Taylors to use laminated backs and sides, and the lines were eventually expanded into a full series of acoustic and acoustic-electric models. Production of the 100 and 200 Series started at the factory in El Cajon, California, and was later moved to Taylor's facility in nearby Tecate, Mexico. With their affordable prices and Taylor-typical playability, the guitars quickly became a huge success with both beginning and experienced players.

2015 *TAYLOR 110ce*

THE TAYLOR GUITAR BOOK

■ Taylor released its own pickup system, which it developed with help from audio legend Rupert Neve, in 2003. Using two top sensors and a magnetic pickup embedded into the NT neck's pocket (middle right), the Expression System also featured a low-impedance preamp (top right) that ran on a pair of AA batteries (right). Discrete controls were placed in the side of the guitar's upper bout area (seen, top, alongside the fingerboard inlay of a 2003 John Denver Commemorative Model).

and was designed to sense the vibration of the strings. But while other magnetic pickups installed in acoustic guitars were typically quite visible, either retrofitted into the soundhole or mounted to the end of the fingerboard (as on Gibson's J-160E), Taylor took advantage of the extended neck pocket of its NT neck to completely hide the pickup under the fingerboard extension. "If we hadn't done the NT neck joint, there wouldn't have been a place to hide a magnetic pickup," Hosler says of the importance of the guitar's integrated design.[57]

The other two pickups of the ES were two transducers mounted to the inside of the top around the bridge area. Rather than using common piezo-based transducers, Hosler developed a pickup based on a wire coil that was suspended inside a round housing, about the diameter of a medium-size coin, and filled with a dampening fluid.

The Neve-designed onboard preamp ran on a pair of AA batteries, which were accessed through a compartment below the endpin-jack. Because the system was designed to be low-impedance for low noise and the ability to run long cables, output was by way of a TRS (Tip-Ring-Sleeve) quarter-inch jack (although the system could be used in high-impedance mode with a standard cable), and it shipped with a special cable that had the TRS plug on one end and an XLR microphone plug on the other for direct interfacing with mixing boards, PA snakes, and so on. The system's onboard controls were kept simple, consisting of just three discrete rotary controls for volume, bass, and treble mounted into the upper-bout area on the side of the guitar.

The Expression System was released to the public at the Winter 2003 NAMM show, replacing the previous stock Fishman pickups on all acoustic-electric steel-strings from the 500 Series on up. If Taylor had already gained a reputation for making great acoustic-electrics over the past decade, having its own proprietary and unique system only strengthened this impression, and reactions to the new electronics were primarily positive. However, while the ES was generally a success, Taylor also learned that developing something outside of its traditional comfort zone includes a steep and ongoing learning curve, and it wasn't long after the first systems had been delivered that tweaks and updates were put in place.

"It was constant for the first four years," Hosler says. Issues ranged from AA batteries getting stuck or rattling inside the barrel that held them in place inside the guitar—Taylor didn't realize that not all battery manufacturers adhered to the exact same diameter—to grounding problems and fluid leaking out of the soundboard transducers. Among the first tweaks was the addition of a dummy coil to the neck pickup, which had been designed as a single-coil, but which users found too noisy. "Rupert thought that we were so low-impedance that we wouldn't have problems with 60-cycle noise," Hosler explains, confirming that many users did indeed report issues with hum and noise.

Virtually every component was redesigned at one point or another to take care of the various issues, but for the next decade, the Expression System's fundamental design and concept remained in place as the standard pickup throughout the Taylor line. (In 2007, the system was switched over to using a nine-volt battery, and in 2010, it changed to using only one body sensor.) Even though the Expression System was designed as a solid stand-alone rig that could feed directly into a mixing board, Hosler and Neve decided to give another powerful tool to players who wanted to take ultimate control over their sound. "We were talking, and I said if I could have anything, I'd have a channel of a Neve console in a box," Hosler remembers. He says they contacted Carnhill in the UK, the manufacturer of the transformers used on may classic Neve preamps. "They still had the specs on the original transformers, so we decided to make up a box."[58] Released in the fall of 2003, the K4 was a stand-alone processor that provided an additional preamp stage, parametric EQ, an effect loop, multiple input and output choices, and more.

Taylor's adventures as it became an electronics manufacturer were taking a lot of energy and resources. But that didn't keep it from developing a new entry-level instrument. Even though Taylor was the company that turned the industry upside down when it introduced its 410 with a price of $998 in 1991, regular price increases had caused the model to break through the $1,500 barrier by 2003. Even the 300 Series now cost considerably more than $1,000, leaving only the not-quite-full-size Big Baby in the realm that competed with a new wave of high-quality imports. These were primarily manufactured in China and sourced by North American companies, such as Saga Musical Instruments and its line of Blueridge guitars.

Even though the Baby and Big Baby had become very successful, they featured a stripped-down design that, while brilliant in its own right, served as a constant reminder of their low cost. "It doesn't matter how the world moves on and prices go up, there is still that line of $1,000," Bob says. "It's almost like that line is magnetic north, and it's not going to move. It doesn't matter: that's the line. As all these other guitars became more expensive through inflation, we had to replace them with something."

The challenge was to create an affordable instrument that looked, felt, and sounded like a "real" Taylor, and the solution was to make them in the Tecate factory over in Mexico, which by now was humming along with the production of cases, Baby Taylors, and Big Babys. "We thought," Bob recalls, "what if we come up with a concept, and the design ethics are: we have two plants, one is in Mexico and one is in the USA. The US guitars become solid-wood guitars—that's the business model that works here—and the Mexican guitars could become guitars that have veneered backs and sides."[59]

The results of Taylor's developments were released as the 110 and the 214 at the Summer 2003 NAMM show. In a slightly odd move, the two instruments introduced two new lines, the 100, featuring laminated sapele back and sides, and the 200, which had solid back and sides (both had solid Sitka spruce tops). But the 100 was only available as a Dreadnought, while the lone model in the 200 "series" was a Grand Auditorium. Even though both guitars cut down building cost by using somewhat simplified construction techniques, including an arched back that didn't require braces and a simplified version of Taylor's NT neck, they were full-size guitars that made good on their promise to deliver the sound and feel that Taylor fans were expecting. At the time of their introduction, the 110 had a list price of $698, while the 214 cost $998. Art Thompson at *Guitar Player* magazine got his hands on an early production model and was bowled over by what the new guitar had to offer. "Among the first

2004 TAYLOR XXX-KE

THE TAYLOR GUITAR BOOK

2004 TAYLOR XXX-MC

 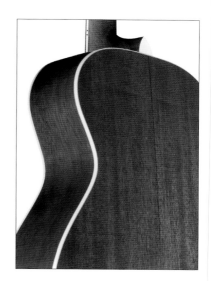

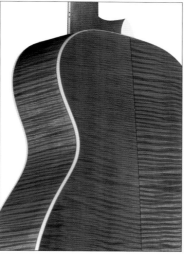 

■ The year 2004 was all about celebrating Taylor's 30th anniversary (Bob Taylor and Kurt Listug pictured then, opposite). This time around, a limited edition run of Grand Concerts that introduced a short scale (of 24⅞ inches) and slotted headstock was offered. They had a special inlay on the headstock rear (opposite) and came in five different wood combinations. They were: Engelmann spruce and Brazilian rosewood (XXX-BE); Engelmann spruce and koa (XXX-KE, back top left, front opposite); cedar and mahogany (XXX-MC, back top right, front left); Sitka spruce and maple (XXX-MS, back above left); and Sitka spruce and Indian rosewood (XXX-RS, back above right).

things you notice about the 110 are how big it sounds and how nicely it plays," he wrote. "In true dreadnought style, its bright, deep voice booms out of the soundhole with cannon-like authority, and you get a palpable kick in the chest when you dig into the low strings."[60]

For the next couple of years, the two models would remain the only representatives of each series, but in 2006, a Dreadnought 210 was added, with more models (including acoustic-electrics) being made available in both Dreadnought and Grand Auditorium sizes in both lines in the years that followed. "The 100 and 200 Series didn't happen until well after Tecate got on its own two feet," Listug says, explaining that to enter a lower-price region wasn't without a risk for Taylor's hard-earned reputation. "They weren't an automatic success just because we offered a guitar at a lower price point. You really have to get the product right, and you have to get the price right, and you have to do the whole job for something to be successful. Just coming out with something cheaper ... you're not going to sell a million of them. Your customers may turn up their noses at it, because it conflicts with their idea of what the brand has come to mean to them."[61]

The year 2004 was all about Taylor's thirtieth anniversary. Amazingly, in the decade preceding this milestone, Taylor's sales rose from about $10 million annually to surpass $50 million. Taylor was now one of the giants of the industry, its approximately 350 employees building more than 70,000 guitars in the previous year. And while the company's founders had a lot of help from an ace staff along the way, it was still run by Kurt Listug and Bob Taylor, who also continued as the sole shareholders of their booming business.

As Taylor had done for its twentieth and twenty-fifth anniversaries, the company decided to offer a special guitar for the occasion. But while previous anniversary guitars brought a completely new body shape (the Grand Auditorium, first offered on the 20th Anniversary model) and the radical new NT neck design (introduced with the 25th Anniversary model), the special guitars created for the company's thirtieth birthday were more subtle from the perspective of new features. "I gave myself a mandate never to have an Anniversary guitar be a 'remake' of something we've already done," Bob says.[62] He decided to use the occasion to introduce something significant, which would show up later in other models.

Using the Grand Concert body platform, the 30th Anniversary guitars were available in five different wood combinations: the XXX-MC (mahogany/cedar), XXX-MS (maple/Sitka spruce), XXX-RS (Indian rosewood/Sitka spruce), XXX-KE (koa/Engelmann spruce), and XXX-BE (Brazilian rosewood/Sitka spruce). Keeping with Taylor's tradition of displaying restraint when it comes to the appointments of its anniversary models, the guitars offered very clean, somewhat understated looks that let their premium woods do most of the talking. They featured the stylized Roman-numeral design in the upper area of the fingerboard that had by now become a tradition. And at first glance, the most unusual feature (for Taylor) was a slotted headstock, something the company had done only for the occasional one-off guitar in the past.

But the most significant news found in the quintet of 30th Anniversary guitars was the fact that they featured a short scale. With the exception of the Baby and a handful of custom guitars, such as a long-neck guitar with a baritone scale built for Dan Crary, Taylors had always featured the industry-standard "long" scale of 25½ inches, regardless of body size. Of course, there is nothing wrong with this choice, as most other makers also use it on guitars of varying sizes. But a number of iconic instruments, such as many Gibson acoustics and all vintage Martins from the 000 down (with the exception of 12-fret 000s and OMs, the latter of which uses a 14-fret 000 body with a long scale), use scale lengths measuring between about 24¾ and 24⅞ inches.

Bob had been experimenting with a shorter scale in response to a request by the Taylor endorser Doyle Dykes, and he was impressed by how the shorter scale (he settled on 24⅞ inches) further eased the effort required to play the guitar. He also found that it delivered a new sound. "This is a tonal change that can only be realized with a shorter string," he explained at the time. "It's not the kind of change, or tonal flavor, that is achieved through bracing."[63] Creating the short-scale anniversary Grand Concerts wasn't just a matter of building a shorter neck and moving the bridge, it also required changes to the top's bracing, such as moving the X closer to the soundhole. This, combined with a slightly increased body depth, completely revoiced the instrument, leaving the way clear for a change to other Grand Concert models.

Beside the set of five short-scale Grand Concerts, Taylor's celebration of its thirtieth anniversary was extended to special commemorative limited editions of every model found in the 300 to 900 Series (designated by the addition of "L30" to the standard model number). They were very similar to standard models but included a special leaf-pattern rosette, some inlay variations, and a "30th Anniversary" script inlaid into the face of the headstock.

The anniversary models' concept of pairing the Grand Concert body with a short scale was eventually applied to all Grand Concerts (first on the 500 Series on up, and later to the 300 and 400 Series). It also resulted in a short-scale version of the Doyle Dykes Signature Model (DDSM), and several limited editions featured the short scale on various Dreadnoughts, including 2005's 710ce-L9, which *Acoustic Guitar* magazine's reviewer described as "great for bending and wiggling strings," adding that it "would be especially loved by players who employ a variety of techniques."[64]

While the hubbub around anniversary models, short scales, and limited editions received most of the attention, several other developments and additions to Taylor's line happened during the same year. Twelve-strings were now offered in the Grand Auditorium size, which was the smallest body to which Taylor had applied this instrument style: previously, twelve-strings were only available as Dreadnoughts and Jumbos. Nylon-string Grand Auditoriums received cutaways, Expression System electronics were extended to 300 and 400 Series guitars, and the Brazilian rosewood Presentation Series was tweaked with abalone binding around the headstock and fingerboard extension.

■

Taylor Guitars had celebrated its thirtieth anniversary and expanded beyond what anyone had dreamt of during the lean early years. By now, it's fair to say there was little left to prove

2007 *TAYLOR T5C-12*

THE TAYLOR GUITAR BOOK

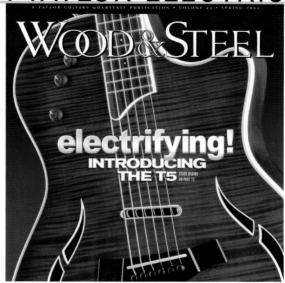

2006 TAYLOR T5 CUSTOM

■ Having gained a good deal of experience through developing the Expression System, Taylor's David Hosler began to experiment with an actual electric instrument. The design ended up as a thinline acoustic-electric hybrid guitar that offered both an acoustic sound with an Expression Pickup and full-on electric sounds with a standard magnetic pickup. Introduced at the 2005 NAMM show, the resulting success of the T5 (above) caught Taylor off-guard at first, leaving the company scrambling to fill orders. A twelve-string version (below) was added in 2007. Originally available in Standard and Custom versions, the T5 line has grown to include a Pro model that's positioned between the two original versions, as well as an entry-level Classic model.

when it came to making a diverse range of excellent acoustic guitars. While nobody had ever questioned that Taylor had revolutionized the way guitars are built, inventions such as the NT neck and the Expression System (ES) electronics had also put the company at the forefront of guitar design and innovation.

And if there is a major advantage of a large manufacturing environment—besides making lots of guitars at reasonable prices, of course—it's that it makes it possible to experiment with new ideas without distracting from what's already taking place.

Having discontinued its line of Steve Klein-designed acoustic basses, Taylor's R&D team around David Hosler was starting to nibble at the idea of creating a new bass design, and before long, a series of thin-body prototypes had been put together. The bass never left the prototype stage, but at some point, Hosler decided to try turning the concept into a guitar. "We took it and put a 110 neck on it," he remembers. "We took a version of the ES system, and made a funny prototype of the guitar. My son Joel, who at that time was on Rick Rubin's label, took the guitar to a gig, and it sounded really good."[65]

At this stage, Hosler thought of the instrument he'd created as a thin-body acoustic-electric that could bring the Expression System's tone to musical settings that required more volume than a full-size acoustic is capable of before feeding back. But then, at another rehearsal of his son's band, the coin dropped on what this new guitar could really be. "Joel and Jon Foreman from Switchfoot were hanging out, and Jon said he wished he had a guitar that could give him some acoustic sounds but also would let him put it in full distortion mode."[66]

What came next were the seeds that would grow into Taylor's immensely successful T5 guitar. Hosler decided to try adding an electric guitar-style stacked humbucker to the Expression System's body sensor and hidden magnetic neck pickup. Before long, he found himself with an incredibly versatile guitar that could cover a huge range of timbres, from amplified acoustic tone to full-on overdriven electric sounds.

It goes without saying that the T5 was different from anything Taylor had ever built. Not much deeper than a Les Paul, the guitar has a body made from sapele wood, and instead of using a separate back and sides, Taylor hollows out a solid piece of wood to create the cavity. The original T5 had a solid spruce top (figured maple or koa were optional), a fully braced and acoustically active design that is bent to a slight arch. The guitar had a mahogany neck with an ebony fingerboard and Taylor's recently introduced short scale of 24⅞ inches. Larry Breedlove designed the archtop-style f-holes to work in harmony with Taylor's standard acoustic ebony bridge.

On the electronics side, the T5 offered a single visible pickup, a stacked humbucker in a chrome lipstick-type cover mounted at a slight angle about an inch and a half from the bridge. This was in addition to a version of the Expression System familiar from Taylor's acoustics, which used another magnetic pickup hidden under the fingerboard extension plus a body sensor mounted on the underside of the top. Rather than placing the guitar's controls in the treble side of the lower bout like on virtually every other electric guitar, Taylor moved the bass, treble, and bass controls familiar from the ES into the bass side of the upper bout, using the same small knobs that are used on the acoustics. A five-way switch mounted into the bass side of the guitar was wired to allow the following pickup combinations: neck pickup and body sensor; neck pickup only; bridge pickup; neck and bridge pickup in parallel; and neck and bridge in series. All together, these combinations covered the range from something similar to Taylor's ES-equipped acoustics through to full-blown electric sounds. The result was definitely more of an electric guitar with an optional acoustic sound than the other way around. In fact, when this book's author requested a T5 for review in *Acoustic Guitar* magazine in 2005, he was told that it wasn't really a good fit, as it was an electric instrument!

Taylor wasn't the first company to attempt to make a hybrid guitar that combined acoustic and electric qualities. Instruments such as Godin's LGX, Hamer's DuoTone, and the Parker Fly all attempted similar feats, in some cases very successfully. But when Taylor showed some prototypes to see what the general reaction might be, the instruments were received with great enthusiasm, essentially blindsiding everyone at the company, including the production team that now had to figure out how to get the actual manufacturing up and running in record time.

"We decided to take it to the NAMM show," Hosler says. "Everybody thought we might make a couple here and there, but the response was huge. We got back to the shop, and Bob said OK, order wood, write programs, buy tools. It was one of the most amazing things I've ever seen happen."

Released as the T5 Standard (spruce or maple top; simple diamond fretboard inlays; chrome hardware) and T5 Custom (spruce, figured maple, or figured koa tops; "spires" fretboard inlays; gold-plated hardware), and with prices starting at $2,598, the guitars were positioned at the premium end of the electric guitar spectrum, which didn't appear to get in the way of the demand they created. "We got them out there, and it was a phenomenon," Listug says. "The first year, we did $10 million worth of sales with those. It was unbelievable."[67]

It seems amusing now, but at the time of the T5's release, the company worried that its new guitar would be misunderstood. It even sent out to its dealers a document called *T5 Demo Thoughts* explaining just how the guitar should be presented to potential customers. "Do not play extended jazz—it positions the product in the wrong light" and "A great player overshadows the product; an average player with the right chops makes the product shine" were among the nuggets of advice included, aimed at sales people who immediately figured that due to the T5's f-holes, it must be a jazz box, or that because it was a hybrid, it could be outperformed by more dedicated instruments.

Of course, many seasoned pros did "get" the guitar, both in terms of its versatility and because of its ability to combine the sum of its parts into something unique. The former Frank Zappa guitarist Mike Keneally said: "For me, the sound of the thick electric tone combined with a crystal clear acoustic tone, on such a beautiful, playable instrument, is really irresistible."[68] As of this writing, in the first half of 2015, the basic T5 concept remains

2015 *TAYLOR 416ce*

2015 *TAYLOR 616ce*

■ After several years of emphasizing Expression System pickups and T5 electric guitars, and generally becoming known as a cutaway-acoustic-electric company, Taylor decided it was time to make a strong acoustic statement. The result was a new body style, called Grand Symphony, which was slightly larger than the Grand Auditorium and voiced for a rich, full, and powerful acoustic sound. The Grand Symphony was also used for Taylor's shortlived high-end R. Taylor line.

THE TAYLOR GUITAR BOOK

GS SERIES

pure acoustic

THE GS SERIES TAKES SHAPE

The T5's sterling rookie season in 2005 has prompted no shortage of frothy speculation regarding fresh developments for 2006. In the broader context of Taylor's electronics advances over the past several years, from the Expression System to the K4, from the T5's versatile pickup system to a pair of new stomp boxes (see page 8), the momentum certainly seems to be surging along the lines of amplified tone.

What might be next on Taylor's design frontier?

Rewind to May of last year. In the immediate wake of the T5's official spring launch, a fresh wave of excitement was spreading as T5 models began arriving at (and quickly exiting) dealers' stores. The factory was steadily increasing production to fulfill the demand. The company's product development group was already actively exploring the second generation of T5 ideas, from different pickup configurations to new color options (see page 6).

Bob Taylor, as the guiding hand of development, had been assessing the T5's trajectory and pondering the R&D focus and possible tooling efforts that would be necessary to lead the company into 2006. A realization came one weekend, and early the following week Bob convened his design team for a product development meeting at which they would begin charting the course for the coming year.

Bob's top priority: to make a strong *acoustic* statement.

"We certainly were riding high on the T5's success, and a lot of people in our product development group were trying stuff," Bob recalls, "but the next direction wasn't clear. And it occurred to me that there was a whole lifetime to make new iterations and let the T5 develop."

Bob told his design group that Taylor owed it to customers to let them know that the company's head was still very much in the acoustic game.

"We weren't going to go away and become the electric guitar company that used to make acoustics," he continues. "Besides, there were still a lot of ideas that we had yet to express with acoustic guitars."

continued on page 16

BY JIM KIRLIN

PHOTOS BY
PPM / PAT BOEMER &
RITA FUNK-HOFFMAN

2008 *TAYLOR 816ce*

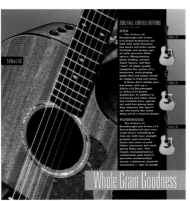

■ To make the point, Taylor initially only made the Grand Symphony style available in its new Acoustic Series, and without pickups or cutaways. The guitar's acoustic tone did impress most players and reviewers who played one, but most customers ended up asking for one with a pickup. So Taylor integrated the style into its standard series, offering both cutaway and non-cutaway versions of the body shape.

2015 *TAYLOR 526*

unchanged, although the Standard and Custom models have been joined by the T5 Pro and the stripped-down T5 Classic. The platform has also been used for numerous limited editions during the decade since its introduction.

■

Taylor had spent much of the past several years developing pickups, establishing its position as a premier maker of acoustic-electrics, and introducing the T5 electric. In 2006, the company took a serious step toward demonstrating that it hadn't forgotten about its core acoustic audience. "We weren't going to go away and become the electric guitar company that used to make acoustics," Bob says. "Besides, there were still a lot of ideas that we had yet to express with acoustic guitars."[69]

The guitars that followed were among the strongest statements of pure acoustic tone that Taylor had ever made. Not only did the splash include a new body shape, which the company called Grand Symphony (GS), it also presented the new guitars as an independent line that didn't adhere to Taylor's standard series. And as if trying to distance them as much as possible from the CE instruments (cutaway, electric) that the company had become famous for, the new models were only available without cutaways.

Measuring 16¼ inches at the lower bout, the new GS body fit in between the Grand Auditorium and Dreadnought. It was similar to the small jumbo guitars that many independent luthiers were having success with, and which were popular with a lot of contemporary fingerstyle players. Designed by Bob Taylor, Larry Breedlove, and Ed Granero, the body shifted the waist toward the guitar's neck, creating a large active soundboard surface. "The goal was to design a guitar that has a deeper, piano-like bass, way more volume, and a good low-end sustain, without ruining the clarity of the mids and the highs," Bob says. "The idea was to start with the concept of the GA and make it more boisterous."[70]

Even though the GS *would* eventually find itself in the standard Taylor model styling, it was initially introduced as one model that was available in four different wood combinations: Indian rosewood and Sitka spruce; Indian rosewood and western red cedar; tropical mahogany and western red cedar; and big leaf maple and Sitka spruce. Taylor chose premium woods for the guitars, and instead of loading the instruments up with inlay, they were designed to let the materials speak for themselves, with relatively austere appointments similar to the existing 500 or 700 Series.

In many cases, guitar makers pair certain woods with more elaborate appointments, often resulting in woods such as mahogany matched with simpler appointments and rosewood with fancier designs, thereby blurring the line of which change caused an increase in price. Taylor decided to price the four guitars almost identically at $2,698, with only the mahogany/cedar version going for $100 less at $2,598. "One reason we've compressed those prices is to let people know that it really is all about the tone with these guitars," Bob explains. "We're not going to say one guitar is way more valuable than another guitar based on the wood. We've broken down the lines of the decoration, so it's not like you have to buy into the idea of a fancy guitar to get the rosewood."[71]

Even though the Grand Symphony made its biggest splash as a Taylor model, it actually started out as the first design for what was going to be a completely new sub-brand that would be called R. Taylor. It was sort of a way for Robert (Bob) Taylor to renew his vows to the *acoustic* guitar. As someone who loves manufacturing, he didn't really mind the fact that he hadn't been involved in the actual building of guitars for some time. But while the upper spectrum of Taylor's model lineup resided at the high-end of what production guitars had to offer, it was impossible to avoid the fact that building more guitars in a week than many smaller companies were making in a year had led to a perception of Taylor as a mass-producer, and which in the eyes of some customers just wasn't able to achieve the same quality as brands with lower production numbers. The scale of Taylor's operation wasn't the only thing that had changed—the 90s had seen a shift in what was perceived as the holy grail in steel-string guitars. While it was once high-end factory guitars such as Martin's D-45, Gibson's J-200, and even Taylor's own 900 and Presentation Series, it was now a growing number of independent luthiers who built the guitars that many aficionados dreamed of.

Of course, as the scores of pro players in every style who used the company's guitars were demonstrating, Taylor had in no way dipped in quality, but it was also true that customers had more choices than ever before. And while the Taylor factory was doing amazing things, a factory of the size it had become does have to make some compromises in order to ensure efficiency and consistent quality. In some cases, companies address a lack of flexibility in their main production environment by offering a custom shop, which is typically an environment that allows the modification of existing models with options such as different neck widths, wood combination, appointments, and so on. But fundamentally, even custom shop instruments tend to follow the same general design, construction, and manufacturing process as stock models.

Taylor and his team came up with an idea. What if there was a shop that built guitars much in the way that small makers were doing it ... *inside* the Taylor factory? A place that would make instruments by hand, using the highest grade of materials, with enough time to do things like taking into account the weight and stiffness of each piece of wood used, and that could utilize construction techniques that were too time-consuming to use in the larger production environment? Ultimately, these ideas lead to the founding of R. Taylor, which would be to Taylor what Lexus was to Toyota—a higher-end variation of proven designs, taking advantage of its parent company's resources, but also offering original elements.

And it is entirely possibly that a touch of ego was involved, too, in trying to compete with the current crop of young lions. "Part of it was that Bob was a little bit jealous of the regard that some of the smaller boutique makers were held in," Listug says. "He wasn't worshipped in the same way as some of these boutique makers, and he thought there are a lot of cool things that he wanted to do that he can't do on Taylor, that it will take a lot more time."[72] Bob says the idea with R. Taylor "was a guitar that we call the Taylor Master-Something Or

2006 *R. TAYLOR STYLE 1*

2008 *R. TAYLOR STYLE 2*

THE TAYLOR GUITAR BOOK

ROBERT TAYLOR, CUSTOM MADE

■ Though it lasted only from 2006 to 2011, the R. Taylor line was an attempt to build high-end guitars in a small shop-within-the-factory environment. As such, the instruments were hand built by a small team of luthiers, who of course had the ability to access the main Taylor factory's vast resources. R. Taylor introduced the Grand Symphony body style (called Style 1, opposite top), later also used in Taylor's standard line. While the guitars featured fundamental Taylor elements, such as the NT neck, their small-shop construction allowed for much greater attention to detail than was possible in a factory environment. Although R. Taylor had standard models, most were custom instruments, often featuring exotic woods. A Grand Concert size Style 2 (left) and a Dreadnought Style 3 were added in 2008.

THE TAYLOR GUITAR BOOK

103

Another. When we showed the first guitars at our product design meetings, we loved it. It was the Grand Symphony body, and Kurt said this is way too important to just be some model we make, it really should be a brand of its own. He said, 'Something like R. Taylor!'"[73]

R. Taylor was launched in 2006, at the same NAMM show as Taylor's Grand Symphony guitars. But instead of being part of the Taylor booth or having its own presence on the main show floor, the guitars were shown by appointment in a nearby hotel suite. Initial marketing material consisted of a simple legal-size piece of heavy paper that was folded in half, and despite the fact that it had Taylor's backing, there was something cool and "underground" about the new brand.

R. Taylor started with a single model, called the Style 1, which used the same body shape as the Grand Symphony. R. Taylor also used Taylor's NT neck, though with a modified headstock shape. From the beginning, the idea was that R. Taylor would take advantage of the Taylor factory's resources and facilities when it made sense to do so, but for the guitars to be built in a separate environment by a small team of dedicated luthiers. Specifically, R. Taylors were designed in collaboration between Bob Taylor, Larry Breedlove, and a young luthier named Ed Granero, who had shown his talents in the Taylor shop. Taylor moved his long-time friend and employee Tim Luranc into the production of the guitars, where he was joined by veteran Taylor builders Keith Greenwood and Eric Larson.

While fundamentally similar to a Taylor Grand Symphony, the R. Taylor Style 1 varied in that it used solid lining rather than standard kerfing to connect the sides with the top and back, it featured lighter-weight construction throughout, and it was built with the attention to detail that can only be accomplished in a small-shop environment where the same builders see every step of the construction process. "With R. Taylor, I'm willing to go thinner with the wood, and take the time that is required," Bob said in 2006. "We trust the people that are working on the guitars, whereas in the factory, there's always a safety margin built in."[74]

R. Taylor also offered two types of bracing patterns, one similar to Taylor's, the other an asymmetrical X-design. While the base price of $4,300 included mahogany, Indian rosewood, or maple back and sides and Sitka spruce or cedar tops, the guitars were true custom instruments in that the customer could choose from any of the vast wood reserves available to Taylor, as well as specify specs such as neck shape, scale-length, string-spacing, appointments, and so on.

The R. Taylor guitars were sold through a separate network of specialized dealers, and reactions in the press were very favorable. For example, the author of this book wrote in *Acoustic Guitar* magazine: "With its combination of upscale woods and craftsmanship, customizing options, refined sound, and relative affordability (when compared with other small-scale custom makers), R. Taylor guitars are bound to make acoustic flattop connoisseurs take notice."[75]

R. Taylor eventually added to its lineup Grand Concert and Dreadnought body sizes (called the Style 2 and Style 3, respectively), and production moved from a small room within the main factory to its own dedicated space in the R&D wing of Taylor's campus. But in

2011, it was decided that the project was more of a distraction than a benefit, and after about 500 guitars built, R. Taylor was dissolved.

Taylor cites difficulty in marketing the R. Taylor brand and confusion about how they were different from Taylors as a major reason why the brand didn't last. "The big mistake was that we're *not* Lexus, and we're *not* Toyota, we're just Taylor, and we don't get to do the same things," Listug says. "For example, Lexus has Lexus dealers, that's one difference. We have retail stores that we try to talk into carrying one or two of these. How successful would Lexus be if there were two Lexuses on a Ford lot? Probably not very successful at all. But I think the R. Taylor is missing, and we need to take its place in another way. I always said that R. Taylor was supposed to be more lutherie, less abalone. The person who buys a Taylor Presentation Series is not the same person that bought an R. Taylor."[76]

In 2007, Taylor continued its spotlight on purely acoustic guitars by separating them from acoustic-electrics as an Acoustic Series, with new model names and an aesthetic taken from the GS's clean lines. This was a way to demonstrate Taylor's commitment to acoustic guitars and to deal with the fact that the majority of its standard models had slowly morphed into "CE" guitars: in other words, cutaways and electronics had become so predominant that people forgot that many models were still available without them, that any model could be ordered without electronics. "The thinking behind it was that you have your base model guitar, say an 810, but we mainly make 810ce's, because that's what the market wants," Listug says. "There was a discussion: are we missing customers or sales because the base model is sort of invisible to them, because we mainly just sell the CE model?"[77]

The result was Taylor's first completely new naming system since the company came up with its original three-digit system thirty years earlier. Instead of the first number indicating the series, the second whether it's a six or a twelve-string, and the last providing info about the body size, the new designations used two letters for the guitar's body size, followed by a single number for its series.

In 2006, the four new Grand Symphony models became the GS5, GS6, GS7, and GS8, indicating wood combinations that corresponded with Taylor's familiar 500, 600, 700, and 800 Series, and a similar concept was applied the following year to Grand Auditoriums (GA), Grand Concert (GC; featuring Taylor's short scale, and slotted headstocks from the 5 series on up), and Dreadnought (DN). GAs and GCs were available in 3, 4, 5, 6, 7, and 8 series, and DNs in 3, 4, 5, and 8s. GA 3, 4, 6, and 8s were available as twelve-strings, designated by the addition of a "-12" to the existing model name (these represented the only acoustic twelve-strings available at the time). No Jumbo-size models were made available in the Acoustic Series. All Acoustic Series guitars shared the elegant simplicity introduced with the GS, which meant they used ivoroid binding, an abalone rosette (black and white rings on the 3s and 4s), and small abalone position-dots in the fingerboard. Acoustic Series guitars weren't available with cutaways, but they could be ordered with optional ES electronics.

Meanwhile, all models with Taylor's traditional numbering system were now only offered as CE versions, meaning they had cutaways and electronics, thereby officially recognizing

2009 *TAYLOR T3B*

Riding on the success of the T5, in 2007 Taylor introduced a solidbody electric with no pretense to acoustic roots. Available as the SolidBody Classic (right), Standard, and Custom (bottom left and right), they combined elements of Fenders and Gibsons into an original design, often using exotic woods. Taylor developed and made its own hardware and pickups, and devised design solutions, such as a hardwood top inset into the body rather than glued on as a slab. Ultimately, the instruments were unsuccessful in the marketplace, and the entire line was discontinued in 2013.

2008 *TAYLOR SOLIDBODY CUSTOM WALNUT*

THE TAYLOR GUITAR BOOK

2008 *TAYLOR SOLIDBODY CLASSIC*

■ While the SolidBody models were shortlived, an electric model derived from the earlier T5 turned into a success. With its solid center, pair of humbucking pickups (and no acoustic pickup), and electric-guitar bridge, the T3 was a fresh approach to a modern semi-hollowbody. The Bigsby-equipped T3B (top left and right) added a Gretsch-type vibe.

2008 *TAYLOR SOLIDBODY CUSTOM KOA*

what the line had organically turned into. The only exceptions to this rule were found in the fact that 810 and 910 models remained as "legacy" acoustic models (as a result, the 810 and DN8 were very similar guitars, differing mostly in their appointments). Some models received cosmetic tweaks, such as the 500 and 700 Series, which returned to abalone rosettes, and the 800s, which now featured maple binding.

Now in its third year of production, the Expression System electronics featured significant updates, including power from a nine-volt battery (replacing the two AAs in the original ES) and a small switch (reachable through the soundhole) that turned off the body-sensor portion of the system, which allowed a different and less feedback-prone voice for very loud playing situations. All standard-series Taylors could still be special-ordered as acoustic versions without electronics, but players who didn't want a cutaway had to go to the dedicated Acoustic Series.

While creating separate categories for acoustic and acoustic-electric guitars seemed like a good idea—and it certainly helped re-establish Taylor as a serious player in the pure acoustic market—the switch confused customers and dealers familiar with the company's traditional naming convention. By 2012, it was decided to leave the new model numbers behind and to return to CE and non-CE versions of standard models.

Another issue concerned the Acoustic Series instruments. They were met with enthusiasm: for example, in a review of the DN4, *Acoustic Guitar* said that "the Taylor impressed with a voice that was at once muscular and refined. Flatpicked single-note lines possessed a wonderful 'round' quality, and strummed chords came across with authority and definition."[78] But for many Taylor fans, having onboard electronics was such an attractive option that they didn't want to do without them. "What ended up happening," Listug says, "was that they all got ordered with cutaways and electronics! That's what customers wanted and what dealers had confidence in, so we did away with those new Acoustic Series model numbers."[79]

■

The renewed emphasis on fully acoustic guitars that was displayed throughout 2006 and in early 2007 went a long way to appease Taylor fans who had begun to feel uneasy about the company's growing reputation as an acoustic-electric specialist and were still confused about what kind of a guitar the T5 was. However, that winter, Taylor introduced a guitar that would further divide the camps. Yes, there was now a solidbody electric. And one without any pretenses of offering acoustic sounds or being a hybrid of any kind. This was pure rock 'n' roll!

Looking like a distant relative of a Gibson Les Paul, the guitar, which was simply called the SolidBody, had a single cutaway, two pickups, a non-tremolo bridge, and a headstock that modified Taylor's standard design with a slightly more pronounced taper. The guitar was available in three models: Classic, Standard, and Custom. With retail prices that started at $1,748 and didn't end at the $3,000 mark, it entered the market at the high-end of the spectrum. While Taylor's entry into the land of Spandex and Marshall amps surprised even those who had started to warm up to the T5, it's worth noting that it wasn't the only company with an acoustic background to perform the guitar-maker equivalent of Bob Dylan at Newport. Indeed, companies such as Breedlove, Collings, Larrivée, and even Ovation were getting into the game, and they all did so at the boutique end of the pricing spectrum. It's equally worth noting that for Taylor, the solidbody electric experiment lasted only until 2013, when the entire line was discontinued. But let's have a look at how this chapter in Taylor's history came about.

The development of the SolidBody got its start when David Hosler and his team began experimenting with ways to create a more electric version of the T5. Applying the know-how about magnetic pickups he'd gained from working with Rupert Neve on the Expression System, Hosler started to build some humbucker-style electric pickups, eventually landing on a design that everyone at Taylor's R&D team thought sounded really good. "We played those pickups and sort of all looked at each other like, wow!" Bob Taylor recalls. "We decided that this was our license to offer a solidbody. Before this, I was uninterested, because I don't like to copy other people's products."[80]

The guitar that resulted was unique in many areas. While the Classic model used a fundamentally standard swamp ash body made from a solid slab of wood, the Standard and Custom models featured chambered sapele bodies with flamed maple (Standard) or figured walnut (Custom) tops that were *inset* into the body rather than being glued on top, as is common with typical Les Paul-style instruments. Taylor used the single-bolt T-Lock neck joint familiar from the T5 to attach the neck, which came with a rosewood fingerboard on the Classic, and ebony on the Standard and Custom models. All had Taylor's 24⅞ inch scale.

Not surprisingly for a company that prefers to avoid becoming a distributor for third-party parts, Taylor came up with its own bridge design. "We don't want to make a guitar that we bolt on other people's hardware to. We can't do it: we can't bring ourselves to do it," Bob says.[81] Originally conceived as a possible option for the T5, the bridge was made out of aluminum and featured a fully adjustable individual saddle for each string. But its most unusual feature was that instead of being bolted to the guitar's top, it clamped to the guitar by extending through the body, connected with a rear piece on the instrument's back.

Taylor's new humbucking pickups came in two configurations: a standard-size exposed-coil design (used on the Standard); and a mini-humbucker-size with chrome covers (used on the Classic and Custom). On the Classic, the pickups were mounted to a Strat-style pickguard, while the Standard and Custom used Gibson-style mounting rings. The pickups connected to a five-way switch that allowed for various humbucker and single-coil combinations, and there was a single volume and tone control—and, yes, Taylor designed its own knobs.

Even though die-hard electric fans may have been skeptical about an acoustic maker's rock'n'roll machine, early notices were rather positive, with the reviewer in *Premier Guitar* saying: "The open-coil humbuckers give the Standard the feeling of a sleeper muscle car dying to find a fast Friday night match race" and "The overall playability and design of these

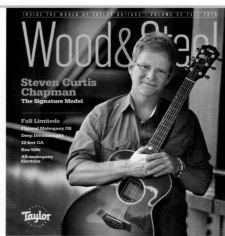

■ By the late 2000s, Taylor's factory had grown to include several buildings along Gillespie Way in El Cajon, California (left). Bob Taylor and Kurt Listug, (seen opposite in front of several of Taylor's CNC machines) continued as sole owners of the company they co-founded almost four decades earlier. Still new guitars and relationships with guitarists were being nourished, including Steven Curtis Chapman, who received a signature model in 2010 (above).

THE TAYLOR GUITAR BOOK

2014 *TAYLOR 812ce 12-FRET*

■ Taylor introduced a 12-fret version (right and below) of the Grand Concert style in 2009. It quickly became a favorite with players who appreciated the design's combination of modern and vintage elements. Moving the bridge further into the lower bout area of the top resulted in a richer tone with a deeper bass response than similar 14-fret models, and the shorter neck yielded greater playing comfort.

2015 *TAYLOR 522 12-FRET*

guitars are top-notch. They are premium solidbody electric guitars from a company who has redefined the acoustic world."[82]

Over the course of the next couple of years, a myriad of options was added to the core SolidBody offerings. In late 2008, Taylor offered the option of a Strat-style single-coil pickup for the Classic, and at the 2009 NAMM show, it expanded on the pickup choice by offering replacement pickguards pre-loaded with various combinations of pickups and controls. Equipped with a simple multi-pin plug, these pickguards allowed players to easily modify their guitar, even combining single-coils and humbuckers, or taking advantage of some variations of different humbuckers that Taylor was now offering with different amounts of gain, tonality, and so on. SolidBody Classics were now also available in a rainbow of colors, from see-through solids to silver sparkles.

Later the same year, at the 2009 Summer NAMM show, Taylor introduced a whammy-bar version of its original bridge, which became an option on all SolidBody models. The bridge used a knife-edge fulcrum design resting on two points, and it was matched with a set of locking tuning machines. While it didn't reinvent the wheel, Taylor's vibrato bridge used a carefully thought out design, and it provided a unique feel by having a lower fulcrum point than most similar bridges. "With traditional tremolos, the fulcrum point is very close to the strings," David Hosler explains, "but we like the feel of lowering the fulcrum point so you have a more balanced, natural feel. It also tends to bring the trem back to a more natural resting position."[83] In 2011, Taylor introduced a double-cutaway version of the Standard and Classic models, thereby creating an instrument that bore some resemblance to a Stratocaster. Materials, pickup and hardware choices, and general appointments were the same as on the original single-cutaway models.

In the end, though, competing with established electric guitar brands in an already crowded high-end field proved to be too difficult for a company that is really known for acoustic guitars, regardless of the immense success that had come with the T5. "Here's the struggle as a guitar builder," Bob says. "There's this discussion that goes around and around, and you can never get off of it, and that's the thing of players wanting something new, something different—that's one side of it. OK, so we give them something new and different, and what they want is a Les Paul and a Strat. Or they want a Martin dreadnought or a Taylor 814ce."

Taylor managed to create a category for itself in acoustic guitars, he continues, that really didn't exist. "We became a company that wasn't venerable, and we became venerable. How does that happen? We thought maybe we can do it again with electrics, but it was really hard, because people loved it, but they really did want to just play their Les Paul or their Strat. That type of thing happened pretty strongly, and so we'd sit down and we'd say well, the thing is, we need something that's *really* different, and I'd say we already do it: it's called the T5! That guitar was successful because it was different and new, and nothing else had been like it."[84]

Kurt Listug concurs about the experience. "I was pessimistic about it. Other people were more optimistic, that we'd sell a lot and that they'd be well received, so we put them out there.

Dealers' expectations for them were misplaced. We had built them a popular brand that had people walk into their stores and ask for Taylor guitars, meaning our acoustic guitars." Dealers, Listug says, thought that because Taylor is so popular for acoustics, people would just walk in and ask for and buy the electrics. "And they didn't. It didn't work the same. After we saw how that played out, I realized that it's a new business: it's really like when we started. Dealers couldn't clerk the sale, they had to do all of the hard work and pioneer that product line. We had to find the dealers that believed in it and were willing to roll up their sleeves and do the hard work, because it wasn't like oh yeah, here's another 814ce, how do I pay for it? There wasn't the demand for it, and you had to work to create the demand."[85]

Though it was introduced after the SolidBody, Taylor's T3 is much more of a close descendant of the successful T5, and as such, it shouldn't be a surprise that it would survive the cutbacks on the company's electric line. Introduced at the 2009 NAMM show, the T3 looks similar to the T5 at first glance, due to its similar body, f-holes, slanted fingerboard extension, and so on. But closer inspection reveals a guitar that has broken away from its acoustic heritage.

Let's start with the obvious. Instead of the T5's wooden acoustic bridge, the T3 sports a Gibson-style stop tailpiece with a roller-saddle bridge. Instead of the five-way switch in the side and the Expression System-style controls in the upper bout, the guitar now had a standard three-way toggle switch and a volume and tone control in the lower bout area of the top. And, most importantly, two of Taylor's full-size humbuckers establish the T3 as a guitar that wants to work an amp rather than pretend it's a full-size acoustic plugged into a PA. Furthermore, the guitar was available (T3/B) with an optional Bigsby vibrato, giving it a touch of the aura of an Epiphone Casino or a Gretsch hollowbody.

There are details under the hood, too, that set the T3 apart from its older sibling. While the T5 has a fully braced, acoustically active top and essentially a hollow body, the T3 has a solid block running down its center, akin to a Gibson ES-335, resulting in a construction that doesn't require braces to support the string tension. The guitar's controls are push-pull units that activate a coil-split function (turning the humbuckers into single-coils) on the volume control, and toggle between a mid-range heavy and a fat jazz sound (achieved with two sets of capacitors) on the tone control. Also, the T3 uses bigger fretwire than the T5 in order to facilitate easier string-bending and other electric guitar techniques.

Though perhaps not as innovative as Taylor's first dip into the electric guitar waters, the T3 was another success, not just in terms of sales but also with the reviewers at guitar magazines. "The prime directive of any semi-hollow electric guitar is versatility," Barry Cleveland wrote in *Guitar Player*. "It should be able to produce woody jazz sounds and punchy rhythm tones, while at the same time being ready to rock at the flip of a switch. The T3/B meets these requirements easily, and greatly exceeds them thanks to its chameleon-like pickups and switching system. The T3/B is about as perfect as a guitar can be."[86] Over at *Premier Guitar,* they wasted no time in putting the guitar on the magazine's cover, and the review was similarly flattering, saying that "the T3/B is not a 'jack of all trades, master of

■ The GS Mini started as an attempt to improve on the Baby Taylor, but it quickly turned into a category of its own. Slightly larger than a Baby, the GS Mini doesn't have the compromised feel of a "travel" guitar. It came with spruce (below), mahogany (opposite), or koa top (right). The GS Minis became instant hits with a wide variety of players, including some physically smaller guitarists who were looking for a great sounding and comfortable instrument.

2010 TAYLOR GS MINI

THE TAYLOR GUITAR BOOK

2009 *TAYLOR BARITONE-8*

2010 *TAYLOR GS MINI KOA*

■ Introduced as part of Taylor's 35th anniversary in 2009, the Baritone-8 (headstock detail above left, and opposite) was perhaps the most unusual model that the company has ever made. Featuring a long baritone scale, the guitar had twelve-string-style octave strings on the third and fourth strings only, creating a huge sound as a result. Also part of the 35th anniversary lineup, but only available as a limited edition, was the XXXV-P parlor-size guitar (pictured in a homely setting, above right). While Taylor has often eventually integrated new body styles into its standard lines, the Parlor was never continued in that way, a fact that has turned it into a highly collectable Taylor model.

2010 *TAYLOR GS MINI MAHOGANY LEFT-HANDER*

none,' but rather a well-thought-out instrument that plays great, sounds fantastic, and looks incredible."[87] In 2014, Taylor would introduce what, at the time of the writing of this book, was its latest electric guitar model. Called the T5z, it was essentially a T5 with a slightly smaller body, though it also had a different fingerboard radius (a 12-inch radius rather than the T5's 15), and jumbo frets, giving it more of an electric guitar feel. The T5z specs mirror those of the standard T5 in terms of woods, appointments, and electronics.

■

Even though 2009 started out firmly in the realm of electric guitars, by the time summer came around, the first rumors of some special thirty-fifth anniversary models started to circulate. Rather than follow a particular pattern that mirrored earlier anniversaries, Taylor chose to celebrate its three-and-a-half-decade existence with a highly interesting mix of special editions and unique guitars, none of which included the Roman-numeral anniversary fingerboard inlay used in previous years.

Staying with the period's electric theme, the 35th Anniversary editions included several batches of SolidBody and T3 models that used highly figured exotic woods. Specifically, the SolidBody was available with tops made out of jaw-dropping feathered koa or highly quilted maple, which was paired with a tobacco sunburst finish. Both top-wood choices were made available for the limited T3 models, which also included an option for dramatically figured cocobolo tops.

Special sets of wood were the main attraction in a limited run of Grand Symphonys, too, which were available with back and sides made out of cocobolo, Macassar ebony, feathered walnut, or quilted maple. The decision to use these particular woods reflected Taylor's position as a company that requires vast quantities of similar wood in order to use it in a standard model. But for a variety of reasons, Taylor also ends up with materials that can only be used in one-off guitars or small runs. Sometimes this is because it will buy a smaller quantity of a certain wood when it becomes available, or because its own grading process might yield more or less random sets that don't match others. "Rather than wait to match these unique wood sets one-by-one with a Build To Order customer, we're going to include them in this special series," Bob said at the time.[88]

The wood used on the special run of 35th Anniversary and Symphonys was spectacular, but the guitars' most significant feature was an element of design. Inspired by the various ergonomic features that had become increasingly popular with luthier-built custom instruments, the guitars introduced a beveled armrest on the bass side of the lower bout, made out of ebony or Indian rosewood. There have been multiple approaches to a similar design, but Taylor was the first large manufacturer to offer this feature, basing its armrest on a design by the renowned Canadian luthier Grit Laskin. (In 2011, the armrest became a standard feature of the Presentation Series, and it also became a custom option; in 2015, it was added to the 900s.)

The most exciting members of the 35th Anniversary family of Taylor guitars were a quartet of instruments that went beyond adding features or special woods to existing models. These models were a Parlor, Baritone, 9-String, and 12-Fret. Let's start with the Parlor (XXXV-P), which may have been the closest Taylor has ever come to creating a guitar inspired by a vintage instrument. Designed by Larry Breedlove, the guitar was about the size of a Martin 0. The Parlor did give a nod to vintage instruments with similar dimensions by sporting a 12-fret neck with a slotted headstock, but it fused this design with Taylor's typical low-profile neck shape and, combined with the guitar's contemporary appointments, the result was an unusually well executed fusion of vintage and modern concepts. It was constructed with Madagascar rosewood for back and sides and a Sitka spruce top (paired with Adirondack spruce braces), and it included a specially designed bridge, with a smaller footprint than Taylor's standard steel-string bridge and a shape that borrowed from the bridge found on Taylor's nylon-strings.

As its name reveals, the 12-Fret (XXXV-TF) also featured a neck joint at the fingerboard's octave, but it did so using Taylor's standard Grand Concert body, essentially creating a steel-string version of the Grand Concert-size nylon-string, which had always come with a 12-fret neck. Built with AA-grade flamed koa for the back and sides (as well as the back of the headstock), an Engelmann spruce top, and an abalone rosette and purfling, the XXXV-TF was a highly elegant instrument. Attaching the neck at the twelfth fret rather than the fourteenth means that the bridge moves further into the lower bout (thus keeping the scale length the same: in the case of the XXXV-TF, that's 24⅞ inches), typically yielding a more robust low-end response. "I've never heard a Taylor sound like this," Bob said of the guitar. "It's warm like a vintage Martin. It's a tone that differs from our regular GC with its distinctive snap and brilliance. It's soft, easy, warm, folky, bassy, and loud."[89] While the Parlor remained a one-off run, making it one of the rarest non-custom Taylors ever made, the 12-fret Grand Concert was a hit, and the configuration was turned into several standard models from the 500 Series on up the following year.

Another 35th Anniversary guitar that would become a standard model (though it ultimately became a custom-order-only instrument in 2014) was the Baritone model (XXXV-B). Taylor had custom-built one-off baritone guitars for artists such as Dan Crary and Dave Matthews in the past, and with the instrument type becoming an increasingly popular option offered by individual luthiers, it made sense that Taylor would want to be among the very few larger companies offering production versions of this kind of guitar. The Taylor's long 27-inch scale is on the shorter end of the baritone guitar spectrum: some feature scales up to 30 inches long. It was designed to be tuned from B to B, a fourth below a standard guitar. Taylor would ultimately offer baritones in other woods as well, but for the 35th Anniversary model, it used Indian rosewood back and sides and a Sitka spruce top on a Grand Symphony platform to create an instrument with a rich low-end rumble.

By far the most unusual instrument rolled out for the anniversary was the 9-String (XXXV-9). "This is for the player who wants some of the twelve-string sound but for whom

■ More players were discovering acoustic baritone guitars, but few big makers offered them. So Taylor included a bari six-string in its 35th anniversary editions. The XXXV-B (below) used a Grand Symphony body and a long 27-inch scale, allowing B-to-B tuning. Baritones were later added to the standard line in various styles. The 35th anniverarys also included Grand Symphonys with exotic woods and an armrest bevel (like the cocobolo XXXV-GS-C, above left), later used on standard 900 and Presentation Series guitars. Dave Matthews got a signature model (opposite), and Taylor's Build To Order or BTO program was going strong, making customer-ordered instruments in every style (above right).

2009 TAYLOR BARITONE XXXV-B

THE TAYLOR GUITAR BOOK

2015 *TAYLOR 418e*

INSIDE THE WORLD OF TAYLOR GUITARS / VOLUME 63 SPRING 2010

Wood&Steel

Dave Matthews
The New Signature Model

2015 *TAYLOR 618*

Spring Limiteds
Koa, Imbuia,
Blackwood & Walnut

Nugent at NAMM
Rocking the T3

Taylor

■ Taylor introduced a new body style in 2013 to replace the old Jumbo shape designed by Sam Radding. Created by Taylor's new luthier Andy Powers, the Grand Orchestra (GO) measured 16¾ inches across the lower bout and was a full five inches deep. A wider waist than that found on most jumbo-style guitars gave it an immediately recognizable appearance (top and right).

a full twelve is too much," David Hosler, the designer of the 9-String, explained.[90] Built with tropical mahogany back and sides and a Sitka spruce top, the 9-String used a Grand Symphony body and Taylor's standard 25½ inch scale, but instead of having pairs of all strings, as a twelve-string would, it had double courses only for the D, G, and B strings. This setup created a hybrid sound that offered a solid dose of twelve-string vibe and tone with significantly easier playability.

Although not part of the 35th Anniversary series, there was another new guitar that was also released in 2009. Clearly developed within the same creative wave that resulted in the Baritone and 9-String models, the Baritone 8-String was perhaps the most unusual instrument Taylor has ever made as part of its standard offerings. Using the just developed Baritone Grand Symphony as a starting point, the Baritone 8-String added octave strings (similar to those on a twelve-string) to just the third and fourth strings. The general concept was not entirely original. The California luthier David Eichelbaum, for instance, had offered standard-scale guitars with a similar string setup as early as 2004. The result was a gigantic sound that expanded on the baritone's low-end rumble with the bright chime of the additional octave strings.

"The beauty of this guitar is that it goes low, and those two strings brighten it up, but they don't sound too octave-y," Bob says. "It doesn't give you that twelve-string effect as much as it really just extends the range, because, as a baritone, the octaves aren't really high. They're not out of the range of a normal sound."[91]

Taylor chose the same Indian rosewood/Sitka spruce combination that it used for the six-string Baritone, and besides the two extra tuners at the headstock and additional bridge pins, the instruments are virtually identical. Most people—including magazine reviewers—who played the Baritone 8-String found themselves agreeing with Bob's enthusiasm. "Taylor has created a unique and unusual instrument for anyone looking for new sounds," Doug Young wrote in *Acoustic Guitar*. "With its extended range and unusual blend of single and double strings, the instrument should excel as a tool for studio work, provide a distinct sound in a song circle or jam, and, above all, inspire new directions for anyone willing to dive in and explore its potential."[92] Art Thompson at *Guitar Player* also gave the guitar two thumbs up. "The Baritone 8-String goes down in my book as one of the most enticing acoustic guitars I've played," he said, adding: "It's practically impossible to not be impressed by everything the Baritone 8-String does."[93]

The period around Taylor's 35th Anniversary had certainly been a creative one. Therefore it's not surprising that 2010 began with a focus on integrating some of the "specialty" guitars introduced with the anniversary, in particular the baritones and 12-frets, into the standard line, as well as offering refinements throughout the line. Taylor also put an increased emphasis on its Build To Order (BTO) program, encouraging customers to make use of its custom shop for anything from special inlays and wood substitutions to completely one-of-a-kind combinations of materials and features.

At the Summer NAMM show in Nashville, Tennessee, Taylor made waves with an inexpensive three-quarter-size guitar it called the GS Mini, with a list price starting at $678.

Using a shrunk-down version of the Grand Symphony body, the guitar features a 23½-inch scale, and while the result was only slightly larger than the dimensions of a Baby Taylor, the new guitar was built with considerations to tone as much as portability. The GS Mini shared elements of the Baby's construction, such as the use of laminated sapele for the sides, a brace-less arched back, and a Sitka spruce top, and it took advantage of the manufacturing know-how the company had gained in the fifteen years since the Baby had been released. As such, the GS Mini featured a full NT neck with a heel; body binding and an inlaid rosette; and a much more refined overall vibe. It was also the first guitar that was designed from the beginning to be manufactured in Taylor's Tecate plant in Mexico, and was therefore never produced in El Cajon.

Almost immediately, the GS Mini's appeal went beyond those who wanted an upgrade from a Baby Taylor. Instead, the instrument found fans with petite players who used it as a main guitar, with students who valued its easy playability, and with pickers who found it to be an ideal couch guitar. Once the reviews came in, they only added to the positive impact the guitar made wherever it was shown. *Acoustic Guitar* said: "With its wide dynamic range, clear tone, long sustain, and affordable price, it's a satisfying and fun guitar to strum, fingerpick, or flatpick and would be a great second—or even first—guitar for any player who needs to have a quality instrument always within reach."[94]

Taylor didn't leave the GS Mini alone. Although initially the guitar was only offered as a purely acoustic model, in order to keep costs down, Taylor offered a clever user-installable pickup as an option. As a magnetic pickup installed in the soundhole, the ES-Go is similar to many aftermarket pickups, but instead of clamping to the edge of the soundhole, it includes a bayonet-style mounting clip that simply slides into a matching bracket that's pre-installed near the neck block of all GS Minis.

"I'd always had this idea that it ought to float in the soundhole and never touch the sides," Bob said of the design, which is a far more elegant solution to installing a pickup in the soundhole than most attempts.[95] The ES-Go is a passive single-coil design, and because Taylor includes a special endpin-jack that can be easily installed from the outside of the body, and which connects to the pickup with a connector equipped with a mini-jack, the entire ES-Go installation can be performed with minimal skills, in a few minutes, and requires only a screwdriver. Players who felt that they needed an onboard volume control could make use of Taylor's new V-Cable, a standard quarter-inch-jack guitar cable that includes an innovative volume control on the back of its angled plug.

■

Thirty-five years after turning the American Dream shop into their own dream, Kurt Listug and Bob Taylor were still at the helm of their company, and they remained as the sole stockholders in Taylor Guitars. They had an enviable combination of complementary skills, a willingness to endure lean years, a work ethic that would have defeated most twenty-

2015 *TAYLOR 326ce*

2010 *TAYLOR BTO GRAND CONCERT*

2014 *TAYLOR BTO JUMBO*

THE TAYLOR GUITAR BOOK

■ Taylor's relatively affordable 300 Series and 400 Series continued to expand. For example, mahogany-top 300s (opposite center) became a popular option for players wanting a tonal alternative to spruce. While twelve-strings were once the sole domain of Taylor's Jumbo bodies, they were now also available in more compact sizes, including this 456ce model (left) from the 400 Series.

2015 *TAYLOR 456ce*

■ As Taylor continued to grow, not only did output increase, but the range of instruments offered also expanded greatly. One area that had become increasingly popular was Taylor's BTO (Build To Order) program, essentially an advanced custom shop. The two highly customized instruments pictured (opposite far left and opposite right) were ordered by Gryphon Stringed Instruments in Palo Alto and are examples of how a creative dealer or individual could get a Taylor like no other. Custom instruments were also a popular choice with mainstream superstars such as Taylor Swift (above).

somethings, and a dose of luck that led to a company which had grown beyond their wildest imaginations. Amazingly, there was still a core group of employees whose relationship with Taylor had started at the very beginning, forming a nucleus of what the company was about. But now, some of these old friends were preparing to retire, and with key partners such as Matt Guzzetta and Larry Breedlove ready to move on—Guzzetta would retire in 2012, Breedlove in 2014—it was time to think not only about the future of Taylor but also about how to make Taylor the best place it can be in the shorter term.

Bob Taylor recalled how the process of looking ahead in earnest began at the company's fortieth anniversary party at the 2014 NAMM show in Anaheim, California. "About five years ago, I sat down with Larry Breedlove, and I said Larry, when are you going to retire? He said in about five years. I said oh-oh, I need a guitar builder, because I'm aging, and I don't want to go back to the workbench. We literally discussed the thing of: what are we going to do?"[96]

Taylor's factory was, of course, teeming with talent, but nobody from within the organization provided an obvious choice to be groomed to lead the company into the future. For some entrepreneurs in Taylor's position, the answer would lie in the next generation of the family, but neither of Taylor's daughters had chosen to follow their father's path. "They're not involved with guitars in any way, which is completely fine with me," he says. "I never viewed this as a family thing. This is the way I wanted to spend my life: not my dad's, and not my kids'."[97]

What Taylor was looking for was somebody who would not just take over guitar design duties from long-time creative spirits such as Breedlove, but also lead the company into its next phase. As odd as it may seem to bring on a new employee who will, as Bob told me, "eventually own the keys to the place," that was essentially what he was looking for. It was not an ordinary search for an employee. "The only thing I knew was to make a list and to ask God," he says. "I literally wrote down on paper: 'Dear God: I need one guitar builder. He needs to be a way better builder than I am. He needs to be self-taught. He needs to know guitar history way deep. He's got to be a pro player.'" Naturally, Taylor was also concerned about investing a lot of time and trust into an unknown person, and he even came up with some additional ideal requirements, which he called "ridiculous." "He has to have twenty years of experience. He has to be less than thirty years old. And he has to be from San Diego, because we don't build East Coast guitars."[98]

Whether it was due to divine intervention, savvy head hunting, or sheer luck, Taylor would ultimately find a young luthier who met all of the points on his wish list, even the "ridiculous" ones. A San Diego native, Andy Powers had been a musician all his life. He began building guitars as a kid—using tools owned by his dad, a professional carpenter—and by the time he was in his mid-twenties, he'd become a respected builder, with a clientele of pro players and a waiting list that spanned several years. Powers was a pro player, with a degree in music from the University of California, San Diego.

Bob and Andy had (unknowingly) met years earlier, and of course Powers was well aware of Taylor Guitars. But it was through Andy Powers the guitarist rather than Andy Powers the luthier that the two would ultimately connect. Powers had been playing with the rising San Diego singer-songwriter star Jason Mraz, a gig that would include a performance at Taylor's NAMM booth in 2010. "His dad was there," Bob recalls, "and he says actually, you met Andy when he was seventeen years old. We sat behind you at a Harvey Reid concert, and he was making a ukulele, and he tapped on your shoulder and asked you questions about it for half an hour before the concert started. I thought wow, yeah, I remember. You're the guy who makes those archtops that people say are so good."[99]

Around this time, Bob had met another highly talented young luthier, Pepe Romero Jr., son of the legendary classical and flamenco guitarist Pepe Romero. He'd tapped into Romero as a source of information for designing a future Taylor classical guitar. Thinking that Romero and Powers would likely hit it off, Bob scheduled what both he and Powers describe as a man-date, where each of them brought a guitar they'd built. "We had like an eight-hour bro-mance that day," Bob recalls. "The next day, I'm driving to work, and I'm sitting at a stop light, and I think Andy Powers, hmmm … my mind went to that check list, and I checked every single box that I had listed!" Bob gave some thought to what he'd experienced, and then he asked Powers whether he'd be interested in working together. Powers remembers the moment, too. "A couple of weeks later," he says, "I got this cryptic email from Bob, saying come down to the shop. Alone. We got together, and he sort of laid out his dream of working together, of doing this."

As enticing as the idea was of working for Taylor in a high-profile position, Powers knew that doing so would require shutting down his own flourishing business, and it took a period of soul-searching before he agreed. "I thought about it for a couple of months. I didn't see it coming, that's for sure," he says.[100] During a transition period, Andy Powers, Pepe Romero Jr., and Bob Taylor worked on prototyping some classical guitars (which as of the writing of this book haven't resulted in a model), Powers finished up his own backlog of orders, and eventually Powers moved into his own workshop, which was located in the former R. Taylor section of the factory.

His job? To make every Taylor an even better guitar than it already was. "Andy is the best guitar maker I've ever met," Bob says. "He's got within him the ability to make guitars sound better. I can't describe it any more than that."[101] Powers in turn says: "I still want to build guitars that are going to allow musicians, whether they know three chords or are reinventing the repertoire for the instrument, to contribute to their artistic vision. Only it's on a far broader platform now."[102]

Andy Powers warmed up by building some one-off Taylor custom guitars, offering some suggestions for design tweaks here and there, designing some new inlays—that kind of thing. His first major project was to create a completely new guitar that was to replace the existing Jumbo size. The last remaining design that could be traced directly to the American Dream, Taylor's Jumbo had continued to use the shape inspired by a Gibson J-200 that Sam Radding had drawn four decades earlier. Redesigning it would be no small feat, as it bore symbolic as well as logistical consequences. "We always felt that we don't make Martins, Gibsons, or

2014 *TAYLOR 150e*

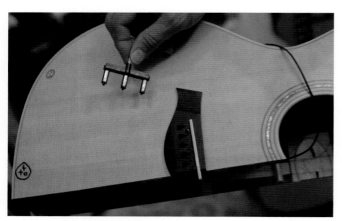

■ Coinciding with Taylor's 40th anniversary in 2014, luthier Andy Powers (opposite top) began to redesign the company's entire line. The first models to be reworked were the venerable 800s, which not only received tweaks in their appointments but also got optimized bracing and wood thicknessing, thinner finishes, and more. The new 800 Series (below) also introduced a new pickup system that would eventually replace the original Expression System throughout. The ES2 (left) uses a three-pronged piezo-based pickup mounted behind the guitar's saddle, while keeping the original Expression System's onboard controls. Taylor manufactures the ES2 components in-house, using robot technology (oposite). Continuing to grow its entry-level line, Taylor came out with its most affordable twelve-string ever, the 150e (above). Also, it expanded its 200 Series (214ce, opposite centre). And with the electric model lines, Taylor built upon its T5 offerings by introducing the smaller-bodied T5z (opposite below).

2014 *TAYLOR 816e*

2015 *TAYLOR 214ce*

2014 *TAYLOR T5z PRO*

Guilds, we make Taylors, and it was time for us to walk away from that Jumbo, even though it was *our* Jumbo," Bob says.[103] At the same time, Powers was feeling that the existing Jumbo shape didn't provide the best platform for what he was trying to accomplish. "I'd been building a bunch of custom Jumbos for a few different players, and I would be trying some ideas," he says. "But at a certain point, I was like, well, I don't really like this shape."

Starting from scratch, Powers drew up a new shape using a less pronounced waist, which he feels helps to make the top more active and effective in tone production. "It opens the whole guitar up a lot. It makes the shape a lot less stiff, because whenever you have tight curves and you glue something to it, it makes a very stiff structure," he explains.[104] He also made the body quite deep, measuring almost five inches at the lower bout, so even though the outline looked a bit like a larger version of the familiar Grand Symphony, the actual internal body volume was quite similar to the larger-appearing Jumbo size.

The new guitar was called the Grand Orchestra (GO), and it was given the designation "8" as the last digit of its model numbers. When Taylor released the new instrument at the 2013 NAMM show, it did so in a similarly limited-edition fashion as it had with other introductions of new body sizes.

Specifically, the Grand Orchestra was first made available as three First Edition models, which included a 518e (mahogany/spruce), 618e (maple/spruce), and 918e (Indian rosewood/spruce). The First Edition was limited to a hundred instruments of each model, which included ES electronics but no cutaways. Later in the same year, the First Edition of Grand Orchestras was expanded with a K28e (koa), 718e, and 818e (both Indian rosewood/spruce). The following year, the GO would be integrated into the standard line, adding cutaways on many models.

The Grand Orchestra replaced the Sam Radding-designed Jumbo that Taylor had been building for thirty-eight years, and it signaled a new era for Taylor in another important way. In Powers's words, it "marked the departure from a one-size-fits-all mentality."[105] Indeed, while it's a somewhat simplified way of looking at it, it's fair to say that, until now, the question "how do we build guitars?" overruled certain specifics of "how are the guitars built?" As a result, once a body style had been designed, it was treated virtually the same, regardless of the woods used in its various models. In other words, elements such as bracing, thickness of tops and backs, and other important elements were applied the same across the board. Given the variation in wood stiffness, density, weight, and so on, it quickly became clear that a more individualized approach would likely yield more fine-tuned results.

With the Grand Symphony, Powers began implementing a much more individualized design approach that involved optimizing each model and then continuing the various design tweaks in the production environment. With Taylor's level of production numbers, this meant major changes along every step of the way. Where, in the past, woods where thicknessed to the same specs across guitar styles, they now had to follow stricter specs. And where there were once bins of pre-shaped braces to be used for every model in a certain body size, the workflow now involved much more variation.

Once the Grand Orchestra line was up and running, Powers began a process where he took a critical look at each of Taylor's existing lines, with the ultimate goal of revamping every model offered. He began by redesigning what could be considered Taylor's most sacred ground, the 800 Series, and as of the writing of this book, the process was far from over. "He's good at preserving what you love about your Taylor: the even, brilliant sound that speaks out when playing with other instruments," Bob says. "But he's also putting more flavor into them. It's good, I must say!"[106]

The revamped 800 Series, unveiled at the 2014 NAMM show during a special fortieth anniversary reception, is an example of Taylor further improving an already proven, successful, and popular product while staying within the perimeters of an existing body shape. And while each of the models in the series received individualized attention, three areas provided key ingredients throughout the line: reshaped braces; optimized wood thickness; and thinner finish. Specifically, Andy Powers lightened up most of the top bracing to some extent, and he also used tapering rather than Taylor's traditional scalloping when he felt that it would yield better results.

The biggest visible bracing change came on the smaller Grand Concert and Grand Auditorium models, which featured back braces that were positioned in a slanted arrangement, rather than the standard ladder braces that meet the sides at a ninety-degree angle. For Powers, this is part of making the top and back work together with the same efficiency that he'd worked out during the design of the Grand Orchestra. "Since I wasn't going to alter the body depth on those models, I wanted to find a way to maintain that same relationship I'd worked out," he says. "After experimenting with some different ideas, I realized that I could change the internal tension of the back by changing the position of the braces a little."[107] He also started using small braces in the sides of the guitars, which he feels helps stiffen the rim and thereby maximize movement of the top and back.

Examples of the same species of wood can vary in density, weight, and stiffness, so thicknessing is best done individually, piece by piece—which is difficult to do without a significant safety margin in a large production environment like Taylor's. But Powers found that he could bring down the margins on certain models, especially the smaller ones. "Because of its smaller outline, the Grand Concert is inherently a stiffer body," he says. "By making the parts a little thinner and more flexible, we can maximize what a player can get out of that guitar."[108] In a move that would appear more in line with a maker of vintage-inspired instruments than the company that spearheaded countless modern manufacturing techniques, Taylor started to use protein glues, such as traditional hide glue, for several building steps. "It's one of those small refinements that, by itself, doesn't make much of a difference, but I've noticed that when you start combining different small refinements, they play off each other," Powers explains, adding that he appreciates the strong adhesion qualities of these glues and their extremely hard curing qualities.[109]

Among the changes that were bound to have an impact across all Taylor instruments was the development of a finish that is almost half the thickness of what had been the standard.

2015 *TAYLOR 656ce*

2015 *TAYLOR 914ce*

2015 *TAYLOR 320e-SEB*

■ In 2015, Andy Powers continued his efforts to re-evaluate every one of Taylor's existing series. The big news for the year was a completely revamped 600 Series (656ce, top), which put an emphasis not only on acoustic tone but also on using maple as an ecologically friendly wood. Powers also put his stamp on a new 900 Series (914ce, above), which now featured an armrest-bevel and similar changes in construction to the 800s the previous year. Later in 2015, Taylor released special-edition shaded-top 300s (320-SEB, above left) and a run of Grand Auditoriums using special woods and featuring a sharp Florentine cutaway (714ce-S LTD, below).

2015 *TAYLOR 714ce-S LTD*

THE TAYLOR GUITAR BOOK

2015 TAYLOR 614ce

Using the same UV-cured polyester material Taylor had sprayed for years, the new finish averaged about 3.5 mils (one mil is equal to .001 of an inch), while the company's standard gloss finish came in at about 6 mils. It's no secret that a finish that's thicker and heavier than it needs to be is likely to impede a guitar's tone, so combined with the other refinements to the new 800s, this step was a major contribution to a more open tone, and it's likely to find its way into other models. "Reducing our finish by almost half and preserving gloss was one of the hardest things we've ever done," Bob Taylor says.[110]

A decade after first introducing the Expression System, Taylor used the opportunity of its fortieth anniversary and the introduction of the revamped 800 Series to introduce a completely new pickup. Even though lots of players loved the sound of the original ES, there had also been a constant murmur from guitarists who felt that it had too much of a magnetic-pickup quality for their liking. And while the bugs that plagued the first editions of the system had long been ironed out, the original ES used a lot of components, which meant that Taylor was still dealing with a considerable amount of customer service issues. But ultimately, coming up with a new pickup may have had as much to do with David Hosler's tireless desire to tinker as it did with an actual need for something new.

While the original ES relied entirely on magnetic technology for its two types of pickups, the ES2 represented a return to bridge-mounted piezo elements. However, while virtually all other bridge pickups place the piezo pickup elements under the saddle, or integrate them in another way that makes them sense an up-and-down motion of the saddle as it is excited by the strings, Hosler placed the sensors behind the saddle. Coming up with this simple yet radically different approach to pickup placement came in the form of an epiphany. "I was looking at a guitar in the repair shop," he says, "and I started thinking, you know what? Our approach to piezos might have been wrong all along. What if the movement at the saddle really is side-to-side, and not up-and-down? That's when it started."[111] Hosler began to experiment by placing a standard piezo pickup element in a routed slot behind the saddle, instead of in the bottom of the saddle slot where it was intended to go. He was encouraged by the results. "Not only did it balance better, it was like twice as loud!"

Enlisting Taylor's long-time industrial design guru Matt Guzzetta (for whom the ES2 would be his final major project before retiring), Hosler came up with a three-pronged pickup assembly that reached through a trio of holes drilled right behind the saddle, between the first and second, third and fourth, and fifth and sixth strings. A copper-covered piezo sensor on each prong touched the back of the saddle, adjusted for optimum pressure with a small Allen-head screw. Though visible from the outside, the system is very unobtrusive, and even though it's essentially a single-source pickup, it provides a combination of string and body sounds in its overall signal.

While the original Expression System's magnet and coil-based pickups could be manufactured using relatively simple equipment, making the ES2 with consistent results and at the necessary speed required research into tools that were new even to the high-tech savvy Taylor. The solution presented itself in the way of small-scale robotics: specifically, a pair of

Epson three-axis robots. Designed to be programmed to assemble small and intricate parts (watch makers use similar machines), these robots were able to handle the tricky combination of materials and small components used in the ES2. "Part of the challenge of folding the copper around the assembly is that the copper is rigid," Hosler says, "and it has conductive adhesive glue on it. The minute I peel the backing paper off of it, I can't touch it."[112]

Even though the preamp used by the ES2 is a completely new design, it is controlled by the same arrangement of knobs (for volume, bass, and treble) as the original ES, mounted into the side of the guitar's upper bout. Similarly, the combined strap-button and battery compartment assembly (with a nine-volt battery) remained the same.

Asked how he would summarize the difference between the ES2 and the original ES in terms of sound, Hosler says: "First, the ES2 is probably more dynamic; and second, its ability to accurately translate what it is that's happening on the guitar is definitely better. It's probably translating what is actually happening on the guitar top and through the resonance better than anything we've ever done."[113] Taylor felt so strong about the new ES2 that the company not only included the system on the new redesigned 800s but also on all acoustic-electrics from the 500 Series on up, starting with guitars shipped in early 2014, adding 300s and 400s in 2015.

■

Taylor builds up to 700 guitars each day and has more than 800 employees spread across the world, so its use of resources has become significant. But just as the minds behind Taylor have been forward-thinking about how guitars are built, they've also made great efforts in reducing the environmental impact. As a matter of fact, in many instances, guitar design, construction methods, and a reduced environmental impact have gone hand-in-hand.

For instance, using a UV-cured polyester finish that's applied by a robot is far less toxic than spraying a traditional nitrocellulose lacquer by hand, but it has also resulted in a more consistent and superior finish overall. Similarly, the fact that switching to the NT neck design made it possible to use 4-by-4 beams rather than quartersawn slabs greatly reduced the amount of mahogany, sapele, and maple required to build Taylor guitars, while also making it easier to acquire high-quality materials.

It goes without saying that Taylor's methods of procuring woods have evolved along with the company. For starters, the general infrastructure of guitar resources looked vastly different in 1974 than it does today. In Taylor's early days, there was no such thing as specialty suppliers and brokers who deal exclusively with the musical instrument trade, so the team had to visit regular lumberyards or buy woods out of the trunk of someone's car. Today, virtually any wood is just a phone call or mouse-click away, and Taylor has of course developed well-established relationships with a variety of vendors.

Taylor has also gone to significant lengths to become involved directly at the source of many of its woods. Collaborating with an organization named GreenWood in Maine, Taylor established in 2000 a presence in the tiny village of Copén in Honduras, which ultimately resulted in much of the mahogany it uses being responsibly harvested and coming from a known source. Taylor invested money to get families in the village set up with updated equipment and trained them to cut and resaw logs for the company's specific needs. Taylor has also worked extensively as part of the MusicWood Coalition, which was founded by Greenpeace and also includes Fender, Gibson, Martin, and Yamaha. The Coalition's goal has been to promote sustainable harvesting of Sitka spruce in Alaska, where the needs of the paper and lumber industries have led to vast areas of clear-cutting.

By far the most far-reaching efforts Taylor has taken when it comes to sourcing its own wood began when the company partnered with the Spanish wood supplier Madinter Trade to purchase its own ebony lumber mill in Cameroon in 2011. To understand why Taylor would risk investing heavily in a business in a third-world country where corruption is the norm and working conditions are difficult, it's important to look at the state of sourcing tropical woods that are integral to guitar construction.

"Ebony has been a wood where, for 200 or 300 or 400 years, we've gone into countries and used the ebony until it's all gone. Then we move into another country and take their ebony until it's all gone," Bob explains. "The last great place to get ebony was Madagascar. It's probably where the ebony that people think of as the true ebony is grown: jet black, perfectly hard. But you know what? It's illegal to cut it there now. The only place where ebony exists is in national parks, and there was a tremendous amount of poaching, to the tune of 200 logs a day literally being stolen out of national parks, destroying habitats—all illegal. For us, it's off limits. We don't buy it. There is one place in the world left where good ebony comes from, and that's the country of Cameroon in Western Africa. Now, do we want to do to Cameroon what we did to Gabon, to the Congo, or to Madagascar, or to Sri Lanka? Or all the other places where ebony grew? In reality, it's the last frontier. There is no other place to go."

While it doesn't get as much attention as some of the more exotic woods used for a guitar's back and sides, ebony is used for the fingerboards and bridges of every Taylor guitar, as well as most other high-quality acoustic guitars. In addition, it's used for the fingerboards and tailpieces of virtually every violin-family instrument. In other words, ebony is an important part of most stringed instruments.

Of course, Taylor-Listug-Madinter (the full name of the partnership) is only interested in harvesting and exporting ebony in a completely legal and corruption-free manner. "We have legal permits done above board, without a penny of bribery or any of the other shenanigans that go on around there, to cut 75 percent of the ebony that's cut legally in the country of Cameroon," Bob says. The partnership has invested heavily into updating facilities, including shipping in from Germany a Unimog truck with a custom-made portable saw mill, as well as sending container loads of tools and materials from the USA.

There was a much bigger lesson in store than learning to work in an environment completely different than anything Taylor had been involved with so far. For centuries, instrument makers had the luxury to use only the darkest, blackest examples of ebony, and as a result, musicians have come to expect just that. But over the course of the last decade or so, pitch-black ebony with no streaks had become increasingly difficult to acquire, and when Bob took a trip to observe how his ebony was being harvested in Cameroon, he found that the impact of consumers preferring "perfect" ebony was worse than anyone had realized.

It's impossible to tell the color of the wood until an ebony tree is felled, so it takes Cameroonian workers an average of ten attempts to find a tree that provides the solid black wood. And because of the effort required to transport trees from the forest to the mill, examples not deemed perfect were simply left to rot, as they weren't going to yield the necessary profits.

Knowing that these differences are purely cosmetic—lighter colored or streaky ebony is just as dense and hard as black ebony—Taylor realized that it was time to change his company's attitude toward using ebony with "character." He's hoping that others will follow and also take up the idea. "We'll do everything we can, as a guitar factory, to make every guitar beautiful," he says, "but the nature of what we thought was beautiful for hundreds of years is simply going to change."[114]

In 2015, Taylor took another bold step toward making its operation less reliant on materials with shady provenance and woods that are difficult or impossible to reliably source in a sustainable manner. The company reinvented its maple-bodied 600 Series. Taylor's use of maple goes all the way back to the American Dream days, and its 600 Series guitars had typically been pushed either for their beautiful looks or as stage guitars, where their somewhat neutral sound worked well for amplification.

Now, Taylor wanted to create a maple guitar that offered the rich, three-dimensional tone typically associated with tropical woods, and the project became a focal point for Andy Powers once he'd completed his work to revamp the 800 Series. He accomplished the new goal by building the guitars lighter, redesigning their bracing, and using torrefied Sitka spruce tops. (Torrefying is a process that simulates aged wood through heat treatment.)

The result was a line of guitars that turned heads at the 2015 NAMM show. "Traditionally, we'd take a guitar that we designed for rosewood or mahogany, take the rosewood or mahogany away, and put maple in its place," Powers says. "Then we'd complain that it's too bright. Well, of course it's too bright. Maple doesn't work the same way!"[115] The results impressed *Guitar Player's* Art Thompson, who reviewed a 614ce model and wrote: "Taylor's Maple Series instruments should go a long way toward changing the mindset of people who think that maple is too bright sounding, and that great tones can only be attained using endangered tonewoods."[116]

Moving forward, Taylor's plans for using maple and other sustainable woods go beyond sourcing the materials from existing forests. Taylor is working closely with Steve McMinn of Pacific Rim Tonewoods, its longtime supplier of spruce, and is actively working on growing future supplies of maple in Washington State, collaborating with researchers at Simon Fraser University in British Columbia, Canada, to learn how to propagate maple that's ideal for guitars. Similarly, Taylor and McMinn have begun a project of growing koa on the Big Island of Hawaii, and as of 2015, there are plans to experiment with growing mahogany and even ebony in Hawaii's tropical climate.

"There are lots of people who are saying that they're using sustainable woods," Bob says. "But I can tell you: I work in Africa, I own a business there, and there's a big difference in doing work there, no matter how great you make it, and what you could do in [the United States]."[117] Of course, the fruits of this labor won't be seen for years, but Bob feels that being part of the solution is an important aspect of the project. "We're looking ahead a century, but with a real business plan. We have to do things on purpose to make up for the failure to do things in the past. It's one thing to tell your supplier not to cut any illegal wood; it's on another level when you're growing the wood for the future."[118]

Taylor took on another gigantic undertaking in 2011 when it set up in Amsterdam in The Netherlands its own European center for distribution, warehousing, and service, from where it now serves the entire European market. The move has resulted in a significant growth of overseas sales. And Taylor's operation in Tecate in Mexico continues to grow, thanks to the success of its entry-level models. For example, in 2014, the 150e was the bestselling twelve-string, while the 214ce was the bestselling acoustic-electric under $1,000 in the USA. In early 2015, the company began moving into a new 116,000 square foot building at the Tecate location. With its lease on the El Cajon facilities coming up for renewal in the near future, Taylor is even looking at the possibility of moving its headquarters and main manufacturing facility from its current location.

It's clear that Bob Taylor hopes that these developments will allow guitarists to enjoy high-quality acoustics for generations to come: developments such as embracing ebony that looks different from what we're used to, and providing guitars like the new 600 Series as part of a game-changing new breed of instruments. And just as Taylor is refining some of its existing lines of instruments, the company is also refining how it operates.

"We're not in a huge technology phase right now, so the things I'm going to talk about aren't as sexy."[119] That's how Bob Taylor responds in the opening months of 2015 to a question about changes to the factory. However, that's not to say that huge things haven't been happening in the way Taylor operates. Bob mentions how much better the company's employee training program has gotten, and how employee health is being looked after in numerous ways, which includes the hiring of an on-site chiropractor.

Kurt Listug agrees about how Taylor has improved in terms of how the company handles its employees. "A big part of what's going well now is that our HR department has matured," he says. "It used to be that if you were faced with someone who didn't work out, it was like oh man, what am I going to do now? How am I going to find someone who is better? What do I do in the meantime? If I lose them, then I don't have anyone to do *that* work! We've been able to upgrade some of the key positions here with people with more experience. We're making greater strides in sales and marketing than we have in many years, and when you have more capable people, it's more fun, too."[120]

More than forty years after they stumbled into careers driven by passion, Bob Taylor and Kurt Listug show no signs of winding down their involvement with the company they founded. "I'm happiest right here," Bob says. "After forty years, it has become so rewarding. Why would I leave? My colleagues here amaze me with their talent, and I have something to offer them because of my experience and my nature to push forward. As an active owner, I can make their ideas for Taylor Guitars possible."[121]

Not surprisingly, Kurt also values the people who have dedicated years of their working lives to make Taylor the success that it is. "I'm really proud that Bob and I have created a solid company that people want to work for throughout their careers," he says.[122] It would be too easy to say that the two of them really did buy the American Dream when they purchased a little guitar shop in San Diego, because what they got was so much more.

I asked them in the spring of 2015 what they thought about recent developments, and they each answered true to their individual characters. "One of the hardest parts of a guitar, one that takes a huge amount of understanding to get it right, is cutting nut slots," Bob laments. "That can make or break a guitar, and it's something that we're seriously considering automating with vision systems and a robot, so that it can be fast. We have to do this thing maybe 600 times a day, and you're trying to teach people the sensitivities of that, you're trying to get them to not cheat it. We're thinking that that might be the next big robotic thing."[123]

Without a doubt, Kurt is also aware of the importance of nut slots—but they may not keep him up at night googling for automated vision systems. However, even after four decades, he's fired up about coming to work, whether in El Cajon or representing Taylor around the world. "I think Bob and I are both really excited about the business, and part of the business remaining to be fun is that HR part," he enthuses. "Because when business turns out to not be fun any more, a lot has to do with the people. So I think it's really important to recognize that and make the changes when you need to, to keep it fun."[124]

Ultimately, then, Taylor is all about fun. Guitarists having fun playing Taylor instruments. Listeners having fun hearing the music. And builders having fun innovating, designing, and creating new guitars. Maybe it is the American Dream after all.

ENDNOTES

1 Simmons *Taylor Guitars*
2 Simmons *Taylor Guitars*
3 Simmons *Taylor Guitars*
4 Author's interview July 30 2014
5 Author's interview July 30 2014
6 Author's interview May 20 2014
7 Author's interview January 30 2015
8 Author's interview July 30 2014
9 Author's interview January 30 2015
10 Author's interview July 30 2014
11 Simmons *Taylor Guitars*
12 Simmons *Taylor Guitars*
13 Simmons *Taylor Guitars*
14 Author's interview May 20 2014
15 Author's interview May 20 2014
16 Author's interview January 30 2015
17 Author's interview May 20 2014
18 Author's interview May 20 2014
19 Author's interview May 20 2014
20 Author's interview May 20 2014
21 Author's interview May 20 2014
22 Author's interview January 30 2015
23 Simmons *Taylor Guitars*
24 Author's interview January 30 2015
25 Author's interview August 11 2014
26 Simmons *Taylor Guitars*
27 Author's interview August 15 2014
28 Author's interview August 11 2014
29 Author's interview August 15 2014
30 Author's interview August 11 2014
31 Author's interview January 30 2015
32 Author's interview August 11 2014
33 Author's interview January 30 2015
34 Taylor *Guitar Lessons*
35 Taylor *Guitar Lessons*
36 Taylor catalogue 1990
37 Author's interview August 11 2014
38 Author's interview August 11 2014
39 Author's interview January 30 2015
40 Author's interview August 11 2014
41 Author's interview January 30 2015
42 Author's interview August 15 2014
43 Author's interview August 11 2014
44 Author's interview August 11 2014
45 Author's interview, August 11 2014
46 Author's interview August 11 2014
47 Simmons *Taylor Guitars*
48 Simmons *Taylor Guitars*
49 Simmons *Taylor Guitars*
50 Author's Acoustic Guitar roundtable discussion January 22 2005
51 *Wood & Steel* Winter 2002
52 *Wood & Steel* Spring 2002
53 *Wood & Steel* Winter 2002
54 Author's interview August 11 2014
55 Author's interview November 11 2014
56 *Wood & Steel* Winter 2003
57 Author's interview November 11 2014
58 Author's interview November 11 2014
59 Author's interview February 3 2015
60 *Guitar Player* August 2003
61 Author's interview January 30 2015
62 *Wood & Steel* Spring 2004
63 *Wood & Steel* Spring 2004
64 *Acoustic Guitar* November 2005
65 Author's interview November 11 2014
66 *Wood & Steel* Spring 2005
67 Author's interview February 3 2015
68 *Wood & Steel* Spring 2005
69 *Wood & Steel* Winter 2006
70 *Wood & Steel* Winter 2006
71 *Wood & Steel* Winter 2006
72 Author's interview August 8 2014
73 Author's interview January 30 2015
74 Author's interview June 2006
75 *Acoustic Guitar* November 2006
76 Author's interview August 8 2014
77 Author's interview February 3 2015

ENDNOTES

78 *Acoustic Guitar* September 2008
79 Author's interview February 3 2015
80 *Wood & Steel* Fall 2007
81 Author's interview February 3 2015
82 *Premier Guitar* July 2008
83 *Wood & Steel* Summer 2009
84 Author's interview February 3 2015
85 Author's interview January 30 2015
86 *Guitar Player* June 2009
87 *Premier Guitar* April 2009
88 *Wood & Steel* Fall 2009
89 *Wood & Steel* Fall 2009
90 *Wood & Steel* Fall 2009
91 *Wood & Steel* Fall 2009
92 *Acoustic Guitar* April 2010
93 *Guitar Player* December 2010
94 *Acoustic Guitar* December 2010
95 *Wood & Steel* Summer 2010
96 Author's recording: Bob Taylor's presentation at Taylor's 40th Anniversary party, Anaheim, California, January 23 2014
97 *Acoustic Guitar* June 2014
98 Author's recording: Bob Taylor's presentation at Taylor's 40th Anniversary party, Anaheim, California, January 23 2014
99 Author's recording: Bob Taylor's presentation at Taylor's 40th Anniversary party, Anaheim, California, January 23 2014
100 Author's interview November 11 2014
101 Author's recording: Bob Taylor's presentation at Taylor's 40th Anniversary party, Anaheim, California, January 23 2014
102 *Wood & Steel* Fall 2011
103 Author's interview February 3 2015
104 Author's interview November 11 2014
105 Author's interview November 11 2014
106 *Wood & Steel* Winter 2013
107 *Wood & Steel* Winter 2014
108 *Wood & Steel* Winter 2014
109 Author's interview November 11 2014
110 *Wood & Steel* Winter 2014
111 Author's interview November 11 2014
112 *Wood & Steel* Spring/Summer 2014
113 Author's interview November 21 2013
114 The State Of Ebony www.youtube.com/watch?v=anCGvfsBoFY
115 Author's interview November 11 2014
116 *Guitar Player* March 2015
117 Author's interview February 3 2015
118 Author's recording: Taylor press event NAMM 2015
119 Author's interview February 3 2015
120 Author's interview January 30 2015
121 *Wood & Steel* Winter 2014
122 *Wood & Steel* Winter 2015
123 Author's interview February 3 2015
124 Author's interview January 30 2015

"There's never been a better time to be making and playing guitars."

TAYLOR'S *WOOD & STEEL* NEWSLETTER, WINTER 2015

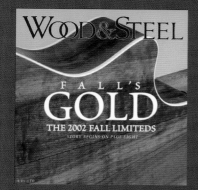 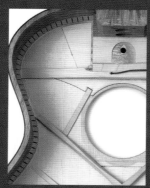  

THE
REFERENCE
LISTING

INTRODUCTION

Taylor's standard guitar models are relatively straightforward to identify, and serial numbers provide accurate information about the year of manufacture (except for the company's very earliest guitars).

Taylor has mostly adhered to a consistent three-digit method for naming its models, providing information about an instrument's series, materials, and size. And while the company has made countless modifications to existing models, it doesn't often introduce completely new models. Many series were established early in its history, and when new body sizes or options have been introduced, they tend to be added to existing lines rather than springing up as completely unfamiliar models.

Since the beginning, Taylor has put paper labels inside the guitar to identify the model and display the serial number. In the case of early instruments, the label will also say whether the guitar was made in Santee, Lemon Grove, or El Cajon. Until 1998, the label was fixed to the neck block. But the label would sometimes be removed or damaged when it was necessary to gain access to the neck bolts during a neck reset (although if the work was done at the factory, the label would be replaced). In 1998, Taylor switched to mounting the label inside the back, using a larger rectangular format with an oval design that varies between standard and limited edition models.

From time to time, Taylor does implement changes within a series to appointments and other details (especially rosettes, binding, and fingerboard inlay), but listing the exact specs and times of each change would be extremely difficult, as even the company's own records are incomplete. However, because the wood combinations used are at the root of each series, identification should be fairly easy, and as long as a serial number is present, dating also should be straightforward. And in most cases there is consistency to a theme: for instance, while 500 Series fingerboard inlays haven't always looked the same, they're virtually always identifiable as a version of small diamonds.

Taylor has regularly offered special editions and guitars with custom specs, ordered in small batches or as one-offs by dealers or individual customers. Because these instruments aren't dedicated "models" as such, identifying them will typically require knowledge of their body size and their woods.

Starting in 2000, Taylor began to offer annual runs of Fall Limited guitars. These are limited editions offered in the last quarter of the year, typically featuring "added value" by using different kinds of woods and more elaborate appointments than standard models. A short time later, Spring Limiteds were added in a similar fashion. Both Fall and Spring Limiteds are variations of standard models, and as such they simply add letters to the regular model name. There have also been numerous short-run limited edition signature models, which are identified on the guitar's label.

Unless otherwise noted, all woods are solid, fingerboards and bridges are made from ebony, and guitars are made in the USA.

The Reference Listing that follows is divided into nine parts.

- **ACOUSTIC MODEL NAMES**
- **ACOUSTIC SERIES**
- **ACOUSTIC BODY SIZES**
- **ELECTRONICS ON ACOUSTICS**
- **ANNIVERSARY MODELS**
- **SIGNATURE MODELS**
- **ELECTRIC MODELS**
- **GENERAL CHANGES**
- **SERIAL NUMBERS**

In the ACOUSTIC MODEL NAMES part, we explain how Taylor's various model-naming schemes work. In ACOUSTIC SERIES, we define Taylor's Series names, and in ACOUSTIC BODY SIZES we define the company's various body sizes (sometimes called styles or shapes). In ELECTRONICS ON ACOUSTICS, we list the various onboard electronic systems that have been available for many Taylor guitars.

The ANNIVERSARY MODELS and SIGNATURE MODELS parts list these special instruments, and ELECTRIC MODELS have their own part, too.

Lastly, GENERAL CHANGES rounds up the global changes made to models that can help identify production periods, while the SERIAL NUMBERS part provides information to help you to date a Taylor by its serial number.

■ ACOUSTIC MODEL NAMES

■ THE THREE-DIGIT SYSTEM

In Taylor's regular three-digit model-name system, the first digit indicates the series, usually representing the first digit of one of Taylor's various series.

For example, a model name with an 8 as the first digit, such as 814, indicates Taylor's 800 Series. For more information on all the series, see the **ACOUSTIC SERIES** section that starts in the right-hand column here.

The second digit is most often a 1 or a 5. A "1" indicates a six-string, "5" a twelve-string. A "2" (six-string) or "6" (twelve-string) means the top wood is the same as the back and sides or is otherwise non-standard.

The third digit indicates the body size. For example, the "4" in our example model 814 indicates size 4, Taylor's Grand Auditorium. For more information on all the sizes, see the **ACOUSTIC BODY SIZES** section that starts on page 147.

A couple of suffix letters can be added to the three-digit model numbers: "C" or "c" means cutaway; "E" or "e" means electronics. So an 814ce means an 814 model with a body cutaway and with electronics onboard.

■ THE TWO-LETTERS-AND-A-DIGIT SYSTEM

A change came in 2006 with new model names for purely acoustic models. These had two letters to indicate body size (DN for Dreadnought; GA for Grand Auditorium; GC for Grand Concert; GS for Grand Symphony) followed by a single number to indicate the series. For example, a model DN8 translated as DN for Dreadnought size; 8 for 800 Series. Twelve-strings added a -12 suffix, for example GA6-12 (Grand Auditorium size, 600 Series, twelve-string). This lasted until 2012, when the regular three-number system—which had continued for models with electronics—was reintroduced across all models, whether pure acoustic or with-electronics.

■ THE OTHER SYSTEMS

ARTIST SERIES models have an A and then two numbers that follow the three-digit system: for example, A55 for a Jumbo twelve-string.
KOA SERIES models have a K and then two numbers that follow the three-digit system: for example, a K10 would be a Koa six-string Dreadnought.
NYLON-STRINGS SERIES models from 2002 to 2012 have NS and then two numbers that follow the three-digit system: for example, an NS62ce would be a Nylon-Strings, 600 Series, Grand Concert, Cutaway, Electric model. Since 2012, Nylon-Strings models use regular three-digit numbers with the addition of an -N, so that example guitar would be a 612ce-N.
PRESENTATION SERIES models have PS and then two numbers that follow the three-digit system: for example, a PS12 model would be a Presentation six-string instrument in Grand Concert size.
WALNUT SERIES models have a W and then two numbers that follow the three-digit system: for example, a W10 would be a Walnut six-string Dreadnought.

■ ACOUSTIC SERIES

■ NUMBERED SERIES
100
2007–current
- Sitka spruce top.
- Laminated ("layered") sapele back and sides.
- Arched back without braces.
- Satin "varnish" finish.
- Black body binding.
- Three-ring rosette.
- Available in Grand Auditorium and Dreadnought sizes.
- Dot fingerboard inlay.
- Twelve-string 150e introduced in 2014.
- Made in Mexico (some very early models made in USA).

200
2007–current
- Sitka spruce top.
- Laminated ("layered") Indian rosewood back and sides.
- Arched back without braces.
- Satin finish.
- White body binding.
- Three-ring rosette.
- Available in Grand Auditorium and Dreadnought sizes.
- Dot fingerboard inlay.
- Made in Mexico (some very early models made in USA).

200 DLX
2014–current
- Sitka spruce top.
- Laminated ("layered") Indian rosewood, koa, or sapele back and sides.
- Arched back without braces.
- Gloss finish.
- White or cream body binding.
- Abalone rosette.

- Available in Grand Auditorium and Dreadnought sizes.
- Small-diamond fingerboard inlay.
- Made in Mexico.

300
1998–current
- Sitka spruce top. (Some models available with mahogany top, indicated by "2" as the second model digit: for example, 322.)
- Sapele back and sides.
- Gloss top, satin back and sides finish.
- Black body binding.
- Three-ring rosette.
- Available in Grand Concert, Grand Auditorium, Grand Symphony, Dreadnought, and Jumbo size. Twelve-string models available in Jumbo and Grand Symphony sizes.
- Dot fingerboard inlay.

400
1991–current
- Sitka spruce top.
- Mahogany (1991–98) or ovangkol (1998–current) back and sides.
- Complete satin finish (1991–98) or gloss top and satin back and sides (1998–current).
- White body binding.
- Three-ring rosette.
- Available in all body sizes. Twelve-string models available in Grand Auditorium, Grand Symphony, Dreadnought, and Jumbo sizes.
- Rosewood (1991–96) or ebony (1996–current) bridge. Pinless bridge (1991–97) or standard Taylor bridge (1998–current).
- Rosewood (1991–96) or ebony (1996–current) fingerboard. Unbound fingerboard (1991–98) or white fingerboard binding (1998–current).
- Dot fingerboard inlay.

500
1978–current
- Sitka spruce, Engelmann spruce, cedar, or mahogany top.
- Mahogany back and sides.
- Some very early examples have rosewood fingerboard and bridge.
- Available in all body sizes. Twelve-string models available in Grand Auditorium, Grand Symphony, Dreadnought, and Jumbo sizes.
- Small-diamond fingerboard inlay (several variations).

600
1978–current
- Sitka spruce top.
- Maple back and sides (high-grade mahogany in 1978 and '79).
- Available with back and sides stained in various colors.
- Available in all body sizes. Twelve-string models available in Grand Auditorium, Grand Symphony, Dreadnought, and Jumbo sizes.
- Variations of "leaf" or "wings"-pattern fingerboard inlay.

Redesigned by Andy Powers in 2015. The new 600s emphasise using maple as a sustainable alternative to tropical hardwoods. At the time of this writing, only available in a violin-like amber stain.

700
1977–current
- Sitka spruce or cedar top.
- Indian rosewood back and sides.
- Available in all body sizes. Twelve-string models available in Grand Auditorium, Grand Symphony, Dreadnought, and Jumbo sizes.
- Dot or small-diamond fingerboard inlay.

The 700 Series has traditionally been Taylor's "value"-minded rosewood guitar. For much of its existence, the series has been a more affordable alternative to the 800 Series. But occasionally, Taylor has positioned the line as having its own identity, as for example in 1998, when it used cedar tops, and in 2013, when it began offering the 700s with sunburst finish and more vintage-style appointments.

800
1975–current
- Sitka spruce top.
- Indian rosewood back and sides (Brazilian rosewood for some early guitars and various special editions).
- Available in all body sizes. Twelve-string models available in Grand Auditorium, Grand Symphony, Dreadnought, and Jumbo sizes.
- White body and fingerboard binding (plastic or light-colored maple).
- Variations on a double-diamond-theme fingerboard inlay.

Redesigned by Andy Powers in 2014.

900
1977–current
- Sitka or Engelmann spruce top.
- Indian rosewood back and sides. (Early 900s had figured maple back and sides, and then switched to rosewood in about 1985.)

- Abalone body purfling.
- Available in all body sizes. Twelve-string models available in Grand Auditorium, Grand Symphony, and Jumbo sizes.
- Elaborate "Cindy" (flowery) or similar fingerboard inlay.

Redesigned by Andy Powers in 2015, adding a Laskin-style armrest and various construction modifications.

■ OTHER SERIES
Alphabetical order

AB1/AB2 (ACOUSTIC BASS)
1995–2002
- Sitka spruce (AB1) or imbuia (AB2) top.
- Imbuia back and sides.
- 19-inch wide wedge-shaped body with cutaway; offset soundhole in treble side of lower bout.
- "Steve Klein" signature inlay in fingerboard extension.
- Asymmetrical pinless bridge.
- Four-strings; 34-inch scale.
- Active Fishman undersaddle pickup with volume and tone controls in side of upper bout.
- Shipped in soft case or gig bag.

AB3 (ACOUSTIC BASS)
1998–2002
- Sitka spruce top.
- Maple back and sides.
- Available in various colors.
- 19-inch wide wedge-shaped body with cutaway; offset soundhole in treble side of lower bout.
- "Steve Klein" signature inlay in fingerboard extension.
- Asymmetrical pinless bridge.
- Four-strings; 34-inch scale.
- Active Fishman undersaddle pickup with volume and tone controls in side of upper bout.
- Shipped in soft case or gig bag.

AB4 (ACOUSTIC BASS)
2001–02
- Maple top.
- Maple back and sides.
- Available in various colors.
- 19-inch wide wedge-shaped body with cutaway; offset soundhole in treble side of lower bout.
- "Steve Klein" signature inlay in fingerboard extension.
- Asymmetrical pinless bridge.
- Four-strings; 34-inch scale.
- Active Fishman undersaddle pickup with volume and tone controls in side of upper bout.
- Shipped in soft case or gig bag.

ACOUSTIC SERIES
2006–12

Introduced with the Grand Symphony body size in 2006, the Acoustic Series was a line of guitars that represented all-acoustic (although ES electronics were available as an option) and non-cutaway versions of Taylor's standard line. Instead of the standard model-number designation, the guitars used two letters to identify the body size, followed by a single number. The letters were DN (Dreadnought), GA (Grand Auditorium), GC (Grand Concert), and GS (Grand Symphony). Numbers used were 3, 4, 5, 6, 7, and 8, which corresponded to the wood combinations used on Taylor's standard 300, 400, 500, 600, 700, and 800 Series guitars. All Acoustic Series models shared a simpler appointments package, which included small position-marker dots in the fingerboard, a single-ring abalone rosette (3s and 4s had plastic rings), and white binding. Twelve-strings were available as Grand Auditoriums in the 3, 4, 6, and 8 series and added the number 12 to the model number, for example GA8-12.

BABY TAYLOR
1996–current
- Solid Sitka spruce or mahogany top.
- Laminated mahogany or sapele back and sides.
- Arched back with no braces.
- Three-quarter-size dreadnought body.
- 22¾-inch scale.
- Made in USA (1996–2005) or Mexico (2005–current).

The Baby Taylor is a three-quarter-size guitar with a short scale that's designed as an easy travel companion or for use by children. At its introduction, two neck-widths were available (1½ inches or 1¹¹⁄₁₆ inches at the nut), but the narrow version was later dropped. Guitars built before June 2001 can be identified by a unique circular brace supporting the top (later models have standard X-bracing). Several special editions have been released, including models with maple, koa, imbuia, or Indian rosewood back and sides, a Liberty Tree version, and a Taylor Swift signature model (see Signature Models, page 152).

BARITONE-6
2009–13
- Sitka spruce top.
- Indian rosewood back and sides (mahogany version added in 2012).
- Grand Symphony body; optional cutaway.

- 27-inch scale.
- Tuned B-to-B.
- ES electronics.

This standard Baritone-6 model was discontinued in 2013, but it is still available as a special order. In 2012, Taylor offered a Fall Limited Edition 416ce Baritone. In 2014, Taylor included a 320e baritone (with all-mahogany dreadnought body) in its Spring Limited lineup. At Summer NAMM 2015, Taylor introduced a limited-edition 326e Baritone-SEB.

BARITONE-8
2009–13
- Sitka spruce top.
- Indian rosewood back and sides (mahogany version added in 2012).
- Grand Symphony body with cutaway.
- 27-inch scale.
- Tuned B-to-B.
- Twelve-string-style octave strings on third and fourth strings only (making a total of eight strings).
- ES electronics.

The standard Baritone-8 model was discontinued in 2013, but it is still available as a special order.

BIG BABY
2000–current
- Sitka spruce or mahogany top.
- Laminated sapele back and sides.
- Arched back with no braces.
- Fifteen-sixteenths-size dreadnought body.
- Standard 25½-inch scale.
- Made in USA (2000–05) or Mexico (2005–current).

DCSM
1986–2000
- Sitka spruce top.
- Indian rosewood back and sides.
- Dreadnought body with cutaway.
- Martin-style diamond fingerboard inlay.

Dan Crary Signature Model. Some early examples have Martin teardrop-type pickguards. Top X-bracing features "straight" rather than scalloped braces.

DDSM
2000–11
- Sitka spruce top.
- Maple back and sides.
- Available in various colors, including natural, black, Gretsch-style orange, and burgundy.
- Grand Auditorium body with shallower than standard depth (4⅛ inches) and Florentine cutaway.
- Gretsch-style thumbnail fingerboard inlay; rose inlay on headstock.
- 25½-inch scale (2000–04) or 24⅞-inch scale (2004–11).
- LR Baggs Hex pickups with six individual brass saddles and side-mounted preamp. (Some DDSMs have standard ES electronics.)

Doyle Dykes Signature Model.

DOYLE DELUXE
2011
- Sitka spruce top.
- Layered maple back and sides.
- Arched back with no braces.
- Black finish.
- Grand Auditorium body with standard Venetian cutaway.
- Gretsch-style thumbnail fingerboard inlay.
- 1¹¹⁄₁₆-inch nut width.
- 25½-inch scale.
- ES-T electronics.
- Made in Mexico.

A low-cost version of the Doyle Dykes DDSM, based on the 200 Series.

GS MINI
2010–current
- Sitka spruce, mahogany, or koa top.
- Laminated sapele, Indian rosewood, or koa back and sides.
- Arched back with no braces.
- Reduced-size GS-shape body.
- 23½-inch scale.
- Made in Mexico.

KOA
Early 80s–current (with interruptions)
- Koa or spruce top.
- Koa back and sides.
- Available in all body sizes. Twelve-string models available in Grand Auditorium, Grand Symphony, and Jumbo sizes.

Taylor used koa as an optional wood very early on, but the Koa Series was officially added to the catalogue in the early 80s. There have been periods where the line was temporarily discontinued due to insufficient supplies of wood for standard production, but it was made available in smaller runs of special editions during those years. Koa Series models use a "K" in place of the typical first number in the three-digit model designation: for example, a K10 would be a Koa six-string Dreadnought. Koa is frequently used for the entire body, although spruce is often substituted for the top.

LKSM-6
1996–2012
- Sitka spruce top.
- Mahogany back and sides.
- Jumbo body with soft Maccaferri-style cutaway.
- Ebony fingerboard with no inlay.

Leo Kottke Signature Model six-string.

LKSM(-12)
1990–2012
- Solid Sitka spruce top.
- Solid mahogany back and sides.
- Jumbo body with soft Maccaferri-style cutaway.
- Ebony fingerboard with no inlay (early models included a "Kottke" signature inlaid at the 12th fret).

Leo Kottke Signature Model twelve-string based on Taylor's 555, but featuring slightly lighter bracing and different voicing to accommodate low tuning with heavier strings. The guitars were shipped tuned to C-sharp, which is the tuning that Kottke uses.

NYLON-STRINGS
2002–current
From their introduction in 2002 until 2012, nylon-string models used the letters NS followed by the first (series) and third (size) number of Taylor's standard numbering system. For example, an NS62ce would be a Nylon-Strings, 600 Series, Grand Concert, Cutaway, Electric model. In 2013, Taylor began using standard model numbers with the addition of "-N," so that same six-string was now a 612ce-N. The same year, the guitars began to feature the same fingerboard inlay and rosette as the steel-string versions of each model, where earlier nylon-strings had a plain fingerboard and classical-style rosette.

PRESENTATION
1996–current
- Sitka spruce top.
- Highly-figured koa, Brazilian rosewood, or cocobolo back and sides.
- Abalone body purfling.
- Available in all body sizes. Twelve-string models available in Grand Auditorium, Grand Symphony, and Jumbo sizes.
- Laskin-style armrest added in 2011.
- Elaborate abalone inlay spanning the length of the fingerboard.

The Presentation Series is Taylor's highest-level standard production model. Presentation Series models use "PS" in place of the typical first number in the three-digit model designation: for example, a PS12 would be a Presentation six-string Grand Concert.

WALNUT
1998–2006
- Claro walnut, spruce, or cedar top.
- Claro walnut back and sides.
- Available in Grand Concert, Grand Auditorium, Dreadnought, and Jumbo sizes. Twelve-string models available in Jumbo size.

Although Taylor had earlier used walnut, the Walnut Series was officially added to the catalogue in 1998, but it was discontinued in 2006. Walnut Series models used a "W" in place of the typical first number in the three-digit model designation: for example, a W10 would be a Walnut six-string Dreadnought.

■ ACOUSTIC BODY SIZES
Within each series, Taylor guitars can be found in six body sizes. These are identified by the last number of the guitar's three-digit model name, as follows.

0 = Dreadnought
2 = Grand Concert
4 = Grand Auditorium
5 = Jumbo
6 = Grand Symphony
8 = Grand Orchestra

A "C" or "c" after the model number indicates a cutaway (upper and lower-case letters were used at different times). For instance, a 614c would be a 600 Series (6) six-string (1) Grand Auditorium (4) with a cutaway (c). Taylor has made significant changes to its Dreadnought body (in 1997) and Grand Concert body (in 2000 and 2004). At the time of writing (2015), the Jumbo is the only body size ever to have been completely discontinued.

0: DREADNOUGHT
1974–current
- Body length 20 inches
- Width at lower bout 16 inches
- Depth: 4⅝ inches

Taylor's original dreadnought shape was designed by Sam Radding at the American Dream and was similar to Martin's 14-fret dreadnought outline. In 1997, Taylor replaced the old design with a new shape that retained the same overall dimensions but which featured more pronounced curves, resulting in a shape that could be described as a blend between Martin's dreadnought and Gibson's slope-shoulder dreadnought. The change was made across the board, with all Dreadnought models from 1997 onward featuring the new shape. Taylor has used Dreadnought bodies for six- and twelve-string models.

2: GRAND CONCERT
1984–current
- Body length 19½ inches
- Width at lower bout 15 inches
- Depth 4⅛ inches (pre-2004); 4⅝ inches (post-2004)

Created in collaboration with fingerstyle guitarist Chris Proctor in 1984, the Grand Concert was Taylor's third body size. While the lower bout is similar to a Martin 000-size, the upper bout is narrower, creating a recognizable original shape. The original Grand Concert shape was redrawn slightly in 2000, resulting in a minimally narrower upper bout and rounder lower bout, and more significantly in 2004, when the 35th Anniversary models increased the body depth by a quarter of an inch to 4⅝ inches and mated the body to a short-scale neck. The change was first implemented on the 500 Series on up and later added to the 300 and 400 Series. In 2009, Grand Concerts became available with a 12-fret neck option. Grand Concerts are available in six-string steel and nylon models.

4: GRAND AUDITORIUM
1994–current
- Body length 20 inches
- Width at lower bout 16 inches
- Depth 4⅝ inches

First introduced with the 20th Anniversary models in 1994, the Grand Auditorium has become Taylor's most popular size. Featuring the same length, lower-bout width, and depth as Taylor's Dreadnought, it has a tighter waist, narrower lower bout, and more rounded curves with fewer straight lines. The Grand Auditorium was added to Taylor's standard models in 1996. One unusual variation of the Grand Auditorium body was found in the Doyle Dykes Signature Model (DDSM), which was made from 2000 to 2011 and featured a thinner body, measuring 4⅛ inches. The body size was made available for twelve-string models from late 2002, starting with a series of Fall Limiteds. The same year, Taylor began using it for nylon-strings.

5: JUMBO
1974–2013
- Body length 21 inches
- Width at lower bout 17 inches
- Depth 4⅝ inches

Like its Dreadnought, Taylor's Jumbo size came from Sam Radding, and it was similar to Gibson's J-200 shape. It was used for both six-string and twelve-string models, but was particularly popular with twelves, and it was the standard body size for this instrument type until the early 2000s. Early Jumbos featured a unique "mustache" bridge design, which continued as an option until 1997. In 2000, the shape was tweaked slightly, with a touch more curve in the lower bout. Taylor discontinued its standard Jumbo size in 2013, but it is still available through the company's Build To Order program.

6: GRAND SYMPHONY
2006–current
- Body length 20 inches
- Width at lower bout 16¼ inches
- Depth 4⅝ inches

Introduced in 2006, the Grand Symphony was originally positioned as Taylor's "pure" acoustic guitar, and as such was initially only available without a cutaway and electronics. The GS also introduced the Acoustic Series, which Taylor offered parallel to its standard-series instruments from 2006 to 2012. The body size was added to the standard line in 2008, and it is available in six-string and twelve-string configurations. Taylor's shortlived R. Taylor brand used the same body size for its Style 1.

8: GRAND ORCHESTRA
2013–current
- Body length 20⅝ inches
- Width at lower bout 16¾ inches
- Depth 5 inches

Designed as a replacement for Taylor's original Jumbo body size, the Grand Orchestra was the first new Taylor created by Andy Powers. Although not quite as wide across the lower bout as the older Jumbo, it has a larger waist and a greater body depth, creating a guitar of similar internal volume. It is available in six-string models.

■ ELECTRONICS ON ACOUSTICS

■ PRIMARY SYSTEMS

Taylor acoustic guitars have included a variety of options for factory-installed pickups over the years, but it wasn't until the mid 90s that the company offered specific acoustic-electric models.

PRE-1998

One of the first standard choices offered in the early 80s was the LR Baggs LB6, a piezo pickup glued to the bottom of a standard saddle element. It remained as an option for many years.

In the early 90s, Taylor switched to various systems based on Fishman's Matrix undersaddle pickup. The base option included only the active Acoustic Matrix pickup (which has an internal preamp mounted to the endpin-jack). A higher-end choice was Fishman's Blender system, which added a miniature internal microphone (made by Crown) mounted to a small adjustable gooseneck, clamped to a top brace. This system required stereo output via a quarter-inch TRS cable and included Fishman's external Blender unit to mix the pickup and mix signals into mono output.

Some limited-edition instruments featured Fishman electronics with two rotary controls (volume and tone) mounted in the upper bout on the side, and several runs of 400 Series models included Fishman electronics with side-mounted volume and graphic EQ controls. During this period, various LR Baggs offerings, including the Ribbon Transducer and Dual Source, were also frequently offered as factory-installed add-ons to standard models.

1998–2003

In 1998, Taylor began offering actual acoustic-electric models by including Fishman Prefix electronics, with preamps featuring volume and EQ controls mounted into the upper bout of the bass side of all cutaway guitars from the 300 to the 800 Series, leading to the addition of "CE" to the guitar's standard model name. The 300 and 400 Series models received the standard Prefix systems, while 500 Series and above featured the Prefix Onboard Blender system, which included a built-in microphone in addition to the undersaddle Matrix pickup. All the Prefix preamps used have a black plastic housing that flips up for battery access and includes a Taylor logo.

2003–2014

In 2003, Taylor introduced its own proprietary Expression System (ES) electronics, which replaced the Fishman systems on all steel-string models. The ES consists of a magnetic pickup that's invisibly embedded under the fingerboard extension, one or two "body sensor" top-sensitive pickups, a preamp with controls for volume, bass, and treble mounted in the bass side of the guitar near the neck's heel, and a combined battery compartment/output-jack/strap-button assembly.

The original ES received invisible updates and improvements throughout its life (particularly during the first couple of years after release), but there are three major versions that featured significant changes.

2003–2006: The original ES1 featured two body sensors and was powered by two AA batteries. Very early systems used a single-coil neck pickup, while later ones added a second "dummy" coil for quieter operation.

2007–2009: The ES1.2 used a new preamp that was powered by a nine-volt battery and included a switch for turning off the body sensors.

2010–2014: The ES1.3 was similar to the previous version but only used one body sensor. As of 2015, this system was still used in the 150e model and was available as a custom order.

2014–CURRENT

In 2014, Taylor introduced its Expression System 2 (ES2). The ES2 uses the same volume, bass, and treble control setup and battery compartment/output-jack/strap-button assembly as the original ES, which means it is not immediately apparent which system is installed in a guitar. But instead of the magnetic sensors for neck and body, the ES2 uses a trio of piezo crystals mounted behind the saddle in the bridge. They are easily identified by the presence of three small Allen-head adjustment screws, which can be seen located between the bridge pins and the saddle.

■ OTHER SYSTEMS
ES-B

Used exclusively in Baby models starting in 2015, the ES-B includes an undersaddle pickup and a side-mounted preamp with volume and tone controls and an onboard tuner.

ES-GO

This is a passive magnetic soundhole pickup designed to be owner-installed on GS Minis sold without a factory-installed pickup. It includes a pickup that snaps into a pre-installed clip on the guitar's neck block and an output jack that installs with three Phillips-head screws in place of the strap-pin.

ES RETROFIT

A version of the original ES designed for installation in pre-NT-neck guitars. The ES Retrofit installs the neck-sensor in a soundhole-pickup-style housing, and for guitars that were previously outfitted with Fishman Prefix preamps, an optional control panel that fit into the existing hole in the guitar's sides was offered.

ES-T/ES ELEMENT

Used on 100 and 200 Series models and GS Minis. Combines an active undersadde transducer with ES-style controls for volume, bass, and treble.

LR BAGGS HEX

A hexaphonic pickup with six individual brass saddles, used on the Doyle Dykes Signature Model (DDSM) in combination with a side-mounted LR Baggs preamp and an output jack in the lower bout, rather than an endpin-jack.

NYLON-STRING MODELS

2002–10: Taylor introduced the Nylon-String series with Fishman Prefix Pro systems. The 300 and 400 Series models had the standard Prefix Pro, while 500s and above used the Prefix Pro Blend, which added an internal microphone to the system's undersaddle pickup. Both systems included graphic EQ and volume controls in the side of the guitar.

2010–CURRENT: In 2010, Taylor began using its ES-N system for nylon-string models. This system combines an active undersaddle transducer with ES-style controls for volume, bass, and treble.

■ ANNIVERSARY MODELS

■ 20TH ANNIVERSARY 1994
XX-MC
XX-RS

- Cedar (MC) or Sitka spruce (RS) top.
- Mahogany (MC) or Indian rosewood (RS) back and sides.
- Large single-ring abalone rosette.
- Non-cutaway Grand Auditorium body.
- Pearl and abalone anniversary inlay (includes "XX") between 12th and 17th frets.
- Limited to 250 of each model.

Introduced the Grand Auditorium body.

■ 25TH ANNIVERSARY 1999
XXV-DR
XXV-GA

- Sitka spruce top.
- Caramel color stained quilted sapele back and sides.
- Wooden rosette.
- Non-cutaway Grand Auditorium (GA) or Dreadnought (DR) body.
- Pearl and abalone anniversary inlay (includes "XXV") between 12th and 17th frets.
- Limited to 500 of each model.

Introduced the NT neck.

■ 30TH ANNIVERSARY 2004
XXX-BE
XXX-KE
XXX-MC
XXX-MS
XXX-RS

- Engelmann spruce (BE, KE), cedar (MC), or Sitka spruce (MS, RS) top.
- Brazilian rosewood (BE), koa (KE), mahogany (MC), maple (MS), or Indian rosewood (RS) back and sides.
- Abalone purfling.
- Non-cutaway Grand Concert body.
- Short scale (24⅞ inches), slotted headstock.
- Pearl and abalone anniversary inlay (includes "XXX") between 12th and 17th frets.

Introduced short scale and slotted headstocks.

■ 35TH ANNIVERSARY 2009

For its 35th anniversary, Taylor introduced 14 limited-edition guitars that combined special versions of existing models and completely new designs. Instead of the large roman-numeral fingerboard inlay used for earlier anniversary models, these models featured a small "35" inlaid in the treble side of the 12th fret.

ARMREST SERIES
XXXV-GS-C
XXXV-GS-M
XXXV-GS-MP
XXXV-GS-W

- Sitka spruce top.
- Cocobolo (C), Maccassar ebony (M), quilted maple (MP), or feathered walnut (W) back and sides.
- Grand Symphony body with Laskin-style armrest in the lower bout.
- Gotoh 510 tuners.
- ES Electronics.

BARITONE
XXXV-B
- Sitka spruce top.
- Indian rosewood back and sides.
- Sunburst top finish.
- Grand Symphony body with cutaway.
- 27-inch scale.
- Tuned B-to-B.
- ES Electronics.

Introduced the baritone to Taylor's line.

ELECTRICS
XXXV-SB-K
XXXV-SB-QM
XXXV-T3-C
XXXV-T3-K
XXXV-T3B-C
XXXV-T3B-K

Single-cutaway SolidBody (SB), with feathered koa (K) or quilted maple (QM) top; single-cutaway semi-hollow with regular tailpiece (T3) or Bigsby (T3B), with premium-grade cocobolo (C) or feathered koa (K) top.

9-STRING
XXXV-9
- Sitka spuce top.
- Tropical mahogany back and sides.
- Grand Symphony body with cutaway.
- Extended headstock with four tuners on bass side and five tuners on treble side.
- 25½-inch scale.
- Twelve-string-style string pairs for second, third, and fourth strings.
- ES Electronics.

PARLOR
XXXV-P
- Sitka spruce top.
- Madagascar rosewood back and sides.
- Non-cutaway parlor-size body.
- Short-scale 12-fret neck with slotted headstock.
- Bridge shape similar to Taylor's nylon-string bridge.
- ES Electronics.

As of 2015, this is the only parlor-size model Taylor has made.

12-FRET
XXXV-TF
- Engelmann spruce top.
- AA-grade flamed koa back and sides.
- Non-cutaway Grand Concert body.

- Short scale 12-fret neck with slotted headstock.
- ES Electronics.

Introduced the 12-fret option for Grand Concert models.

■ SIGNATURE MODELS

CLINT BLACK
CBSM
2000
Grand Concert. Indian rosewood/Engelmann spruce. Presentation Series-like abalone purfling.

JOHN CEPHAS
JCSM
2000
Grand Auditorium. Indian rosewood/Engelmann spruce. Florentine cutaway. "Walking bluesman" fingerboard inlay.

STEVEN CURTIS CHAPMAN
SCCSM
2010
Indian rosewood/spruce Grand Auditorium based on 714. Sunburst finish.

DAN CRARY
DCSM
See Acoustic Series, Other series, DCSM (page 146).

JOHN DENVER
JDCM (COMMEMORATIVE MODEL)
2003
Koa Grand Concert based on K22.

DOYLE DYKES
DDSM
See Acoustic Series, Other series, DDSM (page 146).
DOYLE DELUXE
See Acoustic Series, Other series, Doyle Deluxe (page 146).

RUSS FREEMAN
RFSM
2003
Grand Auditorium, based on 814ce.

SUSANNA HOFFS
SHSM
2003
Koa Grand Concert.

JEWEL KILCHER
JKSM
2000
Grand Auditorium. Satinwood/spruce. Based on 314.

LEO KOTTKE
LKSM-6
See Acoustic Series, Other series, LKSM-6 (page 147).
LKSM(-12)
See Acoustic Series, Other series, LKSM-12 (page 147).

KENNY LOGGINS
KLSM
2000
Koa jumbo.

DAVE MATTHEWS
DMSM
2010
Grand Auditorium, based on 914c. Custom fingerboard inlay includes "Grux."

JASON MRAZ
JMSM
2010
Nylon-String based on NS72ce.

RICK NIELSEN
RNSM
2003
Maple/spruce Jumbo. Stained green or black.

CHRIS PROCTOR
CPSM
2000
Grand Concert. Indian rosewood/Engelmann spruce. 1⅞-inch neck. Florentine cutaway.

RICHIE SAMBORA
RSSM
2000
Koa Grand Auditorium.

TAYLOR SWIFT
TSBT (BABY TAYLOR)
2009–current
Baby Taylor with special rosette.

SERJ TANKIAN
STSM-T5
2010
Black T5 electric with custom inlay.

WINDHAM HILL
WHCM (COMMEMORATIVE MODEL)
2003
Indian rosewood/spruce Dreadnought.

■ ELECTRIC MODELS

■ SOLIDBODY
2008–13
Available in Classic, Standard, and Custom models (plus various limited editions), Taylor's SolidBody models had many shared traits. Available in two versions, a single-cutaway (Classic, Standard, and Custom), and, starting in 2009, a double-cutaway (Standard and Custom only), the guitars used Taylor's own pickups (humbuckers or mini humbuckers, with the Classic also available with single-coils starting in 2008). Controls were for volume and tone, and the guitars had a Strat-style five-way pickup selector switch. The SolidBody originally came with a Taylor-designed fixed bridge; a vibrato bridge was added as an option in 2009. Both bridges offered individually adjustable saddles. The guitars had smaller and more tapered headstocks than Taylor acoustics, and featured 24⅞-inch scales.

* **SOLIDBODY CLASSIC** 2008–13 Solid swamp ash body. Pickups mounted to a Fender-style pickguard. Rock maple neck with rosewood fingerboard. Dot fingerboard inlay.
* **SOLIDBODY CUSTOM** 2008–10 Chambered sapele body, inset figured walnut or koa top. Single- and double-cutaway versions. Pickups mounted to top. No pickguard. Mahogany neck with ebony fingerboard. Progressive diamond fingerboard inlay. Ivoroid purfling.
* **SOLIDBODY STANDARD** 2008–13 Chambered sapele body with inset flamed maple top. Available in single- and double-cutaway versions. Pickups mounted to top. No pickguard. Mahogany neck with ebony fingerboard. Dot fingerboard inlay. Cream purfling.

■ T3
2009–current
The T3s are semi-hollow electrics. They use the same body shape as the T5, but with a solid center-block rather than the T5's completely hollow construction. The body's

back is made from sapele, and tops are maple. The guitars have a Tune-o-matic-style roller bridge with a stop tailpiece (T3) or a Bigsby vibrato (T3B). Electronics consist of two Taylor-brand humbucking pickups (either full-size or mini), a three-way toggle switch in the upper bout section of the top, and a volume and tone control in the lower bout of the top (these are push-pull, providing coil-split and a mid-shift function). T3s are available in a variety of colors.

■ T5

2005–current

The T5 is a hollow-body acoustic-electric hybrid. Its single-cutaway body is 16 inches wide at the lower bout and has a depth of 2.35 inches. The body is made from sapele, capped with spruce, koa, maple, or mahogany tops (cocobolo, Indian rosewood, Macassar ebony, walnut, and ovangkol have also been used). The tops are fully braced, and the guitars have standard Taylor acoustic bridges. Necks are short-scale and have standard-size Taylor headstocks. Electronics consist of a visible "lipstick"-type stacked humbucker in the bridge position (there have also been versions with a second lipstick pickup, which replaces the body sensor), an Expression System-style hidden neck pickup, and a body sensor that's also derived from the Expression System (ES). A five-way switch in the guitar's side allows for various combinations of acoustic and electric sounds. Volume, bass, and treble controls with ES-style knobs are located in the bass side of the upper bout of the guitar's top. The T5 has two highly stylized f-holes. A twelve-string option was offered 2007–14. All are available in a variety of natural, colored, and sunburst finishes.

* **T5 CLASSIC (T5X)** 2010–current. Mahogany top (ovangkol 2010–13). Unbound neck and body. Small diamond fingerboard inlay. Satin finish. Chrome hardware.
* **T5 CUSTOM** (T5-C) 2005–current. Koa top (spruce or maple optional on early models). Bound neck and body. "Spires" or "T5 Artist" fingerboard inlay. Gold hardware.
* **T5 PRO** 2014–current. Flamed maple top. Bound neck and body. "Spires" fingerboard inlay. Chrome hardware.
* **T5 STANDARD (T5-S)** 2005–current. Spruce top (maple optional on early models). Bound neck and body. Small-diamond fingerboard inlay (micro-dots on early models). Chrome hardware.
* **T5Z** 2014–current. A variation with reduced-size body. Other differences include a twelve-inch fingerboard radius (regular T5s have a fifteen-inch radius) and jumbo frets. It uses the same electronics, acoustic-style bridge, and stylized f-holes, and like the T5, it's

available in Standard, Custom, Pro, and Classic versions, with similar woods and features as the corresponding T5s.

■ GENERAL CHANGES

As a company constantly evolving and seeking to improve its products, Taylor has during its history applied countless changes across the board. While some aren't easily visible, and others vary from model to model, there are a few key changes that apply globally, and these can be helpful in identifying when a particular Taylor guitar was manufactured.

■ BRIDGE PINS

The pins of the original Taylor bridge were arranged in a half-moon shape, following the contour of the bridge itself. In 2001, Taylor began to arrange the pins in a straight line, with an equal distance from each pin to the back of the saddle.

■ BRIDGES

Early Taylors had either Martin-style bridges or (less frequently and more often on Jumbo models) "mustache"-shape bridges. The original bridge shape that Taylor became known for, designed by Larry Breedlove, was first used with the Grand Concert and Artist Series models around 1984 and 1985 and became the new standard in 1986. Taylor returned to the earlier shape for the 400 Series in 1991, but in a pinless version. The 400s were upgraded to the standard Taylor bridge in 1998. The mustache bridge remained an option on Jumbo models (both six- and twelve-string) but was last used on a standard production model (an 815) in 1997.

■ CUTAWAYS

Early Taylors had Florentine-shaped cutaways, with a sharp point. Florentine cutaways have remained as custom options (and they've been used on limited editions, as well as the Doyle Dykes Signature Model). But for the most part, Taylor switched to the softer Venetian cutaway in the early 90s. The Dan Crary and Leo Kottke signature models used original cutaway shapes.

■ HEADSTOCK JOINT

NT necks (see also page 154) are made from three separate pieces of wood, including the neck itself, the heel, and the headstock. From the NT's introduction around 2000 until 2007, the headstock was attached using a multi-pronged and sometimes quite visible fingerjoint. In

2007, the design was switched to a more elegant looking scarf joint. Baby Taylors have always had a fingerjointed headstock. Pre-NT necks were one-piece.

■ NECK WIDTH AT NUT

Taylor has offered neck-widths of 1¹¹⁄₁₆, 1¾, and 1⅞ inches throughout its history. Until the arrival of the NT neck, most Dreadnought and Jumbo models had the 1¹¹⁄₁₆ size, Grand Concerts and Grand Auditoriums measured 1¾, and twelve-strings had the 1⅞ version. Six-strings were available with all three sizes by special order. Six-strings with the NT neck from the 300 Series on up now all measure 1¾, regardless of their body size, but the other widths are available by special order.

■ NT NECK

Taylor introduced the NT neck with its 25th Anniversary models in early 1999, and by early 2001, the entire catalogue had been converted to the new design. The first models to be switched were 300 and 400 Series Dreadnoughts, followed by 300 and 400 Series Grand Auditoriums. Twelve-strings and Grand Concerts were the final types to be converted, in early 2001.

■ R. TAYLOR

R. Taylor was the brand for a line of high-end guitars made by Taylor in a "small shop within the factory" environment, from 2006 until 2011. R. Taylor introduced the Grand Symphony body size, which it called Style 1. Base models included wood combinations of mahogany/cedar, Indian rosewood/cedar, Indian rosewood/Sitka spruce, and big leaf maple/Sitka spruce, but custom woods and specs were encouraged. Besides body shapes, R. Taylors shared many Taylor construction traits, such as NT necks, but also differed in details, such as using solid lining rather than kerfing to connect the top and back with the sides, and much more careful wood selection and individualizing of parts than Taylor's standard production environment allowed. R. Taylor headstocks differed from standard Taylors in that they had a slightly less tapered shape. In 2008, a Grand Concert-size Style 2 and a Dreadnought-size Style 3 were added. Designed to compete with instruments made by small companies and individual luthiers, R. Taylors were mostly custom instruments with unique features. The line was discontinued in 2011.

■ TUNING MACHINES

Early Taylors used mostly Schaller and Grover tuning machines. For most of the 90s and early 2000s, standard-size Grover Rotomatic machines were used for all six-string models and Grover Rotomatic Minis for twelve-strings. In 2003, the company switched to its own Taylor-branded tuners, with an 18:1 ratio, for the majority of its models. Presentation Series guitars and some limited editions use Gotoh 510 tuners. Nylon-string and slotted-headstock steel-string models use generic open-gear machines.

■ SERIAL NUMBERS

Taylor has used several systems for serial numbers, and all of them can be used to reveal the date of a particular guitar's manufacture.

■ SERIAL NUMBERS 1975–92

Number range	Approximate year of manufacture
10109–10146	1975
20147–20250	1976
20251–30353	1977
000–467	1977
468–900	1978
901–1300	1979
1301–1400	1980
1401–1670	1981
1671–1951	1982
1952–2445	1983
2446–3206	1984
3207–3888	1985
3889–4778	1986
4779–5981	1987
5982–7831	1988
7832–10070	1989
10071–12497	1990
12498–15249	1991
4-0001–4-1132	1991 (400 Series only)
15250–17953	1992

■ SERIAL NUMBERS 1993–99

From 1993 until the end of 1999, each Taylor guitar featured a **nine-digit serial number** that pinpointed precisely when work was begun on that instrument.

- The first pair of digits represents the last two digits of the year; the second pair represents the month; and the third pair represents the calendar day that work was begun.

- The seventh digit is a Series code number: 0 for 300 or 400 Series; 1 for 500 through Presentation Series; 2 for 200 Series; 3 for Baby and Big Baby Series; 5 for T5; 7 for Nylon-Strings Series; 8 for 100 Series; and 9 for SolidBody Series.

- The last two digits denote the guitar's position in that day's production sequence.

For example, 960416129 indicates a guitar made in 1996 (96), April (04) 16th (16); 500 Series or higher (1); 29th guitar that day (29).

■ SERIAL NUMBERS 2000–09

In 2000, the existing system was expanded to an **eleven-digit serial number** in order to use a four-digit year.

- The first four digits indicate the year; the fifth and sixth digits represent the month; and seventh and eighth digits represent the calendar day that work was begun.

- The ninth digit is a Series code number: 0 for 300 or 400 Series; 1 for 500 through Presentation Series; 2 for 200 Series; 3 for Baby and Big Baby Series; 5 for T5; 7 for Nylon-Strings Series; 8 for 100 Series; and 9 for SolidBody Series.

- The last two digits denote the guitar's position in that day's production sequence.

For example, 20030910103 indicates a guitar made in 2003 (2003), September (09) 10th (10); 500 Series or higher (1); third guitar that day (03).

■ SERIAL NUMBERS 2009–CURRENT

In November 2009, Taylor introduced a new **ten-digit serial number** system.

- The first digit represents the factory: 1 for El Cajon, California; 2 for Tecate, Mexico.

- The second and seventh digits represent the last two digits of the year; the third and fourth digits represent the month; and the fifth and sixth digits represent the calendar day.

- The last three digits denote the guitar's position in that day's production sequence.

For example, 2112034079 indicates a guitar made in Taylor's factory in Tecate, Mexico (2); in 2014 (second digit 1, seventh digit 4), December (12) 3rd (03); 79th guitar that day (079).

INDEX

A page number in *italic type* indicates an illustration. A page number in the range 143–155 indicates an entry in the Reference Listing.

THE TAYLOR GUITAR BOOK

INDEX

ACKNOWLEDGEMENTS

PICTURES

The majority of the images featured in this book were supplied by Taylor Guitars, and we are most grateful for their help and for their permission to reproduce them. The exceptions are as follows, keyed by page number and an abbreviation: GSI = Gryphon Stringed Instruments; TG = Teja Gerken.
66 Bob Taylor with guitar body: TG.
67 NT shims and three factory shots: TG.
102 Two R. Taylor guitars: GSI.
103 Three R. Taylor shop images: TG.
122 2010 Taylor BTO Grand Concert and 2014 Taylor BTO Jumbo: GSI.
126 ES2 pickup: TG.
127 Andy Powers shot, ES2 robot shot: TG.
131 Body sides shot: TG.

AUTHOR'S THANKS

Huge thanks goes to Heather Gould and Sabine Gerken, who supported their husband and daddy during the writing of this book. Big thanks also to Bob Taylor, Kurt Listug, Andy Powers, Chalise Zolezzi, David Hosler, Rita Hoffman, and Jim Kirlin at Taylor Guitars. Furthermore, Michael Simmons, Richard Johnston, Chris Proctor, Sam Radding, Larry Cragg, the staff at Tall Toad Music, Bananas at Large, and Gryphon Stringed Instruments, and my fellow Pegheads, Dan Gabel and Scott Nygaard.

BOOKS

Tony Bacon *History Of The American Guitar* (Backbeat 2011).
Teja Gerken (et al) *Acoustic Guitar: An Historical Look At The Composition, Construction, And Evolution Of The World's Most Beloved Instruments* (Hal Leonard 2003).
Dave Hunter (editor) *Acoustic Guitars: The Illustrated Encyclopedia* (Thunder Bay 2003).
Paul Schmidt *Art That Sings: The Life And Times Of Luthier Steve Klein* (Doctorow Communications 2003).
Michael John Simmons *Taylor Guitars: 30 Years Of A New American Classic* (PPV Medien 2003).
Bob Taylor *Guitar Lessons: A Life's Journey Turning Passion Into Business* (Wiley 2011).
David Russell Young *The Steel String Guitar: Construction & Repair* (updated edition) (Bold Strummer 1987).

TRADEMARKS

Throughout this book we've mentioned a number of registered trademark names. Rather than put a trademark or registered symbol next to every occurrence of a trademarked name, we state here that we're using the names only in an editorial fashion and that we don't intend to infringe any trademarks.

UPDATES?

The author and publisher welcome any new information for future editions. Write to: Taylor, Backbeat & Jawbone, 3.1D Union Court, 20–22 Union Road, London SW4 6JP, England. Or you can email: taylorguitar@jawbonepress.com.

"My first impression of Bob Taylor was oh, he can have a bench in my shop any time he wants. He was well beyond where he should have been, had he been a normal person."

Sam Radding at American Dream makes an assessment of Bob Taylor's early guitar-making skills.

More Great Guitar Titles from
BACKBEAT BOOKS

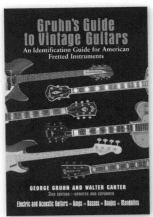
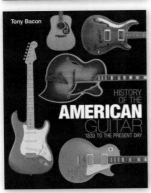
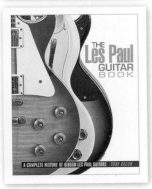